Jennifer's journey in living both a "Whole" and holy life is a great encouragement to those of us in ministry families. "Whole" provides us with fresh biblical insights that will strengthen us all onward.

—*Elizabeth Chotka, Former District Ministry Spouse Coach, C&MA Canada*

This is a read for every woman not just pastors' wives. Jennifer shares bravely her own struggles, captivating the reader and challenging us to live out the life God has called us to live. It is both inspiring and hopeful.

—*Darlene Snider former missionary and pastor's wife*

Whole

Hope for the Broken Pastor's Wife

Debi
Thank you for believing
in this message and
for your endless support
and encouragement!
Jennifer
Willcock

Jennifer Willcock

Unless otherwise indicated, all Scripture quotations are taken from THE HOLY BIBLE, NEW INTERNATIONAL VERSION®, NIV® Copyright © 1973, 1978, 1984, 2011 by Biblica, Inc.® Used by permission. All rights reserved worldwide. • Scripture quotations marked NASB are taken from the NEW AMERICAN STANDARD BIBLE®, Copyright © 1960, 1962, 1963, 1968, 1971, 1972, 1973, 1975, 1977, 1995 by The Lockman Foundation. Used by permission. • Scripture quotations marked MSG are taken from The Message. Copyright © 1993, 1994, 1995, 1996, 2000, 2001, 2002. Used by permission of NavPress Publishing Group.

Printed in Canada

ISBN: 978-1-4866-1418-9

Word Alive Press
131 Cordite Road, Winnipeg, MB R3W 1S1
www.wordalivepress.ca

Library and Archives Canada Cataloguing in Publication

Willcock, Jennifer, author
     Whole : hope for the broken pastor's wife / Jennifer Willcock.

Issued in print and electronic formats.
ISBN 978-1-4866-1418-9 (paperback).--ISBN 978-1-4866-1419-6 (ebook)

     1. Willcock, Jennifer. 2. Spouses of clergy--Biography.
3. Christian life. I. Title.

BR1725.W544A3 2017   270.092   C2016-906678-9
                                             C2016-906679-7

For Michelle Jones
Who knew that our first cup of coffee and a chat about being married to a pastor would result in this book? Thanks for the many cups of coffee over the years and for walking every step of the way with me.

Acknowledgements

It is such a humbling experience to thank the many people over the years who have encouraged me in writing this book. There's a whole community of people who have stood behind me, encouraging, supporting, and praying for me, my family, and this book. Thank you, thank you, thank you.

To the many pastors' wives I've had the pleasure and privilege of serving alongside over the years, thank you for making ministry richer because you were a part of it. I feel blessed for having you in my life.

Thank you to Tia, Lori, and Warren, my team at Word Alive Press. Thank you for your expertise and hard work and for making this book a better read.

Thank you, Jo Lynn Duck. I wouldn't have a book in my hands without you.

Thank you, Darlene Snider, Michelle Jones, Garth Leno, Pat Orser, Mary Hildebrand, and Nicole David, who read all or portions of this book. Your input and cheerleading were invaluable. Your enthusiasm always amazes me. Thank you.

Thank you to Brenda and Robin, my writing partners, who helped me cross the finish line with their encouragement and enthusiasm.

Thank you, Trina, for going to Nashville with me! Unforgettable!

Thank you to Jody and Alex Cross and Paul and Diana Havercroft.

Your continued friendship and mentoring have been priceless gifts! God seems to bring you across our paths at just the right moments!

Thank you, Michelle and Scott, for keeping it real and fun for us! "Live long and prosper!"

Thank you to my mom and dad, who taught me that nothing is impossible with God.

Thank you to Marguerite and Peter, who have done so many things for me so I could have time to write.

Ian and Ben, I love you both more than life itself. You guys make me a better person.

Mark, you have put up with more than any man should have to. Thank you for your encouragement and love and for believing in me when I didn't even believe in myself. Your steadfastness to your call despite everything gives me hope. I love you.

Introduction

Once upon a time, when I'd hear about a young woman who was going to marry a young man who was training to be a pastor, I wanted to send her a sympathy card rather than a wedding celebration card. My heart literally ached for her and what was surely coming.

I assumed that she would be blissfully ignorant of what she was getting herself into and too in love to understand. She wouldn't take it the way it was intended: a message of commiseration and letting her know she wasn't alone. Give it a few short years and, unfortunately, she would totally understand where I was coming from. There was no happily ever after in ministry. Or so I thought.

Cynical and angry—not a great mix in any girl. I thank God that He has changed my perspective—not just about ministry but about life. I'm not the same as I was as a young twenty-something woman, and the changes have permeated through all areas of my life, not just my role of pastor's wife. Not that being a pastor's wife has gotten any easier. In fact, it gets harder with every passing year. The world offers countless distractions and competes for my time, as well as our congregation's. Truth is hard to come by. Wickedness is emerging. It's the world I live in, and God has put me here, in the role I'm in, for this time. But, no, ministry doesn't get easier.

Society is just part of it. If you've lived through any conflict in the church, you know it can be ten times harder. The majority of our almost two decades in full-time ministry has been narrow and rocky. My husband and I experienced two church splits, closed a church, and dealt with many other leadership issues. We've been called bad names. People who we thought loved us have left us, left the church. I could go on. So why then has my perspective changed, improved? Why am I embracing ministry rather than running from it?

Along that narrow and rough path, God showed up. He met me where I was. It wasn't that great a place, but He came anyway. He called me by name. He took my hand and walked beside me—a mess of a girl who didn't have a clue what she was doing.

Along that rocky path, new life was shoving its way up out of the earth. He allowed my heart to break in many different ways and then lovingly put it back together, healing the wounds and hurts. He is still doing so. In dark times, He led the way. He offered hope and encouragement when the way was particularly tough. He never once left my side, and He carried me often. As He put my heart back together, He transformed it to look more like His. Although the way was still hard, my heart remained strong as long as it was attached to His. Hope shone through because He is mine and I am His. He has never let me go. I am not alone.

I don't want to send a sympathy card anymore. I still want to let those young girls know they're not alone, but I want it wrapped up in an encouragement card. To let them know that in the hard times, when the path is particularly full of sharp rocks and stones, hope is still alive. He is alive and well and moving in our lives. He hasn't left us alone. Yes, it's tough. *It's going to be hard!* Our hearts will be broken, many times over.

My own experience as a pastor's wife and ministry leader has led me to believe that life in ministry is meant to be lived out on God's terms and no one else's. This means that there is hope for families of pastors, for their wives, and for the pastors themselves, if they will let God have His way in their lives and in the lives of the churches they lead.

Does this sound harsh? Set aside your preconceived notions. It's not about stereotypes, rules, and regulations. It's about following hard after Jesus and letting Him have His way in your life. It opens up endless possibilities because it throws to the curb all the world's ideas of what matters and lets God, the Creator of the universe, reign in your life! It's breathtaking if you're willing to go there with Him.

God loves His church. He dearly loves those who serve in it and their families. He has a plan. It's been in place since the beginning of time. When the temple was destroyed by the Romans in AD 70, He had already laid the foundation of the new temple with living stones. We are part of that, living stones stacked one on top of each other, according to Beth Moore in her James study, *James: Mercy Triumphs*.[1] First Peter 2:4–5 says, "As you come to him, the living Stone—rejected by humans but chosen by God and precious to him—you also, like living stones, are being built into a spiritual house to be a holy priesthood, offering spiritual sacrifices acceptable to God through Jesus Christ." I was awestruck when I read that, because it shows how much God cares about and loves the church. It has nothing to do with a physical building, but it has everything to do with His people. He had a better plan. And it had everything to do with His love for us. His heart for us. He isn't going to let the church (His people) die and decay. He's moving each one of us into our place. He cares that much about us, about His bride. For many of us, it's going to take a change of heart for us to put our hearts in His big hands and let Him do with them what needs to be done. That's downright scary, but at the same time it's comforting. Healing brings hope.

So I'm here to encourage you. If you feel like giving up, don't—hold on. There's an end coming to these troubles. In the meantime, He hasn't let you go. Grab on to Him. Give your heart to Him and hang on. It's worth it, believe me. I've been there. I understand. It hurts so much. I am writing this to you so you can be encouraged. So that you'll hang on just a while more. Trust Him.

I truly believe that He wants you to hear from Him as you read this. It's His message to you. I've tried to walk away from this so many times, but I can't run away from it. It's too important.

One last thing. There are two pieces of paper that sit in my Bible. Actually, there are many pieces, but these two are special, now a few years old. One is dated March 22, 2009. I was in Nashville at a conference for pastors' wives. We had been singing an old hymn, "How Great Thou

Art"—just the voices of the women. It was incredible. So pure and beautiful. I was thinking to myself that God must be pleased with it. And I felt God whisper in my ear that He was more than pleased. He whispered to me, "These are women I love. You love them too." It brings tears to my eyes as I sit here, years later.

The second piece of paper is from a church service. I've written, "Make it worth it. Make it worth all the suffering. Live extraordinary lives for God and His Glory."

There is hope. Hope in the God you serve. Make it all worth it, sister.

Chapter One

Disappointed

I *wanted to travel. Write. Experience adventure.*

The small farming village I grew up in, where my father has lived all his life, didn't offer the things I craved. My father built our house. By his own sweat. With his own hands. I lived there until I moved away to attend university. Stability and security lived in that house on Coleman Street. I knew my roots. Hidden beneath those roots was a longing for adventure. I had wanted to be a journalist since I was about ten. I chased hard after that dream.

Journalists travel, visiting exotic locations. They see mountains and oceans. They vie for the best position on the steps of courthouses and government buildings. They meet new people, learn about their lives, and tell their stories. It made my young heart leap with joy and anticipation.

It didn't work out the way I envisioned it. I ran after that dream to one of the best schools of journalism in the country. One little grade smashed that dream to bits. I had worked hard, but it wasn't enough. At age twenty, I didn't know how to fight for what I wanted in life. I walked away from journalism with my head bent in shame and defeat. I wasn't enough. Would I ever be?

Although a journalism degree wasn't waiting for me at university, my future husband, Mark, was there, and we met in our last year of study.

We started dating a few months later. I remember one night sitting with him in a coffee shop, talking. He told me he thought he was called to the ministry. He said he believed that God was calling him to be a pastor. I noticed that he was nervous telling me, and I didn't understand why. I told him I was okay with it, although I really didn't have a clue what I was agreeing to. I thought we'd be poor (I knew that much) and I would have to make something out of nothing. I was already well rehearsed in that lifestyle, being a starving student, living on my own. In addition, growing up in a family of seven children, I knew a little about making something out of nothing. I had watched my mom and dad do it all my life. Looking back, if I had had any idea of what was coming, I would have put on my jacket and run far away from that coffee shop as fast as I could! Fortunately, we can't see into the future. A few months later, I agreed to marry a future pastor.

Funny thing—that adventure I'd craved all my life was about to unfold in the wilds of ministry.

Funny thing—that adventure I'd craved all my life was about to unfold in the wilds of ministry. At the time it didn't look like adventure knocking, but in hindsight it was an invitation to enter into the upside-down world of God. The adventure of ministry. I didn't understand it then. It's taken me years to even start to figure it out.

After graduating with an honours English degree, I pursued my own dreams of a career in writing. I wanted to prove that I was good enough. I wanted to make this dream happen. Job leads came and went. Employment promised to me mysteriously disappeared.

I remember having an interview with an acquaintance at his place of work. He was enthusiastic about me joining them. I never heard back. Finally I heard that they weren't hiring. After that, I shadowed a friend of my sister's in a marketing firm. They were friendly and enthusiastic about me working there. The job was ripe for the picking. And then...nothing. No phone call. Silence. They too decided not to hire.

What is wrong with me? became my mantra. I had a degree from university, and it was as useful as a soggy paper towel. I knew deep down that fundamentally there must be something wrong with *me*. I had the tools. It must be me.

Food and shelter were required, so I went to work at the mall, in retail. Not the dream I envisioned. It smacked of boredom and monotony. The pay was minimum. How was I going to support us as my husband got his master of divinity degree?

Disappointed with myself and God, I didn't understand why I kept hitting a brick wall. Blind to the fact that I was following my own agenda and that it was not *His* plan for me, I kept pursuing the dream. Was I supposed to ask God what kind of job He wanted me to do? I was ignorant of the idea of talking to God about my dreams, jobs, and future. It wasn't something I learned growing up in our church. I missed that Sunday school lesson, I guess.

When my husband had earned his master's degree and started his first full-time ministry job, I was still careerless. My dreams had been dashed. Even my lowered expectations had been stomped on. I felt like a nothing. Satan was having a field day, whispering lies in my ear: *Useless. Worthless. Dumb.*

Through the lies, I heard a whisper: *What if his career is also your career?* I knew immediately that this thought was from God. I would never have thought something like it on my own. I stopped. What if I changed my attitude? What if I quit fighting?

"Follow Me, and I will make you fishers of men," Jesus said (Matthew 4:19 NASB). What if I was being called too? Maybe it wasn't a case of "Well, that's his job, and I'll have my own." Maybe God didn't intend it to be that way. Was that why I was always getting a "no" in the career arena? Was I intended for something much more? Perhaps the two of us were supposed to be in ministry together.

It was a pivotal moment. It opened my mind to the idea that maybe I was being called into ministry too. It stopped my perpetual fight against it. It changed my attitude. I still had a long way to go, but the direction I was headed in changed with that one thought. I still believed the lies the enemy was telling me, but I was now moving in the right direction for hope, healing, and a life of adventure.

A PARTNERSHIP

Ministry is all about partnerships—with your spouse, with the church board, and with the congregation. Most of all it's partnering with God in the work He is doing in your realm of influence. God created partnership. He created the first woman and called her to help her husband, Adam. I've had to take Eve down off the cartoon Bible story shelf and re-examine her. Eve was more than the girl who ate the fruit that plunged humanity into sin. God's plans for her were so much bigger.

Eve was the final act of creation. It's interesting to think about. Why was she last? Adam needed a helper, and none of the animals or birds or fish was suitable. Why? Adam needed more companionship than the animals provided. He needed an equal. A partner. God created Eve because He saw it was not good for man to be alone. Adam needed someone to help him, but more than that, he needed a relationship. Someone to talk with about how funny the monkeys were behaving, how beautiful the orchids were, and what was wrong with those vines, anyway? Adam needed a living, breathing, talking helper. Which makes sense, because God is all about relationships. He created man so man could have a relationship with Him.

Eve helped Adam with the animals and the garden. She worked alongside her mate. It wasn't just Adam who was created to be in relationship with God; Eve was too. God's image was part of her too. Ethel Herr, in her book *Chosen Women of the Bible*, says, "Eve's story demonstrates an ideal. It shows God's original design for our place in relation to (1) God, (2) men (especially our husbands), (3) our children."[2] She states, "Woman's place is under her God, beside her husband and before her children, bringing glory to God in all her relationships."[3] The world today makes fun of this priority list, but they've got it wrong.

Hang in here with me for a minute. I know this is a hot topic. I think we've been misled by the standards of the world and what the world wants us to focus on. Distractions keep us from the most important mission of our lives. Social media, busy jobs, and overcrowded schedules keep our eyes to the ground instead of looking up. We just need to get through this one last thing…and then there's the next one thing. It goes on and on.

We're told from a young age that we can have it all. Really? I don't know of a single person who has it all. There's usually at least one thing missing. We race around, desperately grabbing at all the things the world tells us we need. They aren't even bad things. It becomes a juggling act, and near the end all we really want is to let it all fall so we can get some peace.

I don't believe for a second that that kind of life equals having it all. Maybe having an anxiety attack. Maybe having a heart attack. Maybe that's what we need—an attack on our hearts so we wake up to what's really important and become aware of who we are really supposed to be. Relationships with God, with our families, and with our friends—these are why God created us. These give us life in abundance.

We are God's cherished daughters. He wants us to come visit. To talk with Him. To tell Him about our days. Our fears. Our happiness. He loves us. He wants us to love Him back! It says in His Word (Jeremiah 31:3) that He loves us with an everlasting love! Doesn't that intrigue you? The God of the universe loves us with a love that never ends! Nothing can snuff it out. Not anything we can ever do or be. He is calling us to come to Him. Why do we resist?

Why do I hold back? I'm too wrapped up in the shoulds, woulds, and could have beens. Aren't you? We get caught up in all we think we've failed at. We ruminate on what we should have done or didn't do. We focus in on how we aren't making the grade and probably never will be good enough. We think to ourselves, if we could only be *this*, then we would be valuable. Waffling back and forth. I feel I've disappointed not just myself but others who expected that I would make a name for myself. Failure is my name.

I had failed at everything. Writing. Getting a decent job. The lies replayed over and over again. To add salt to the wound, I felt like a loser at being a pastor's wife. Yes, I believed I was called too, but I wasn't like the other women I'd known growing up. I couldn't get this right either. I didn't fit in. It felt like God was setting me up for failure over and over again.

I didn't understand that it wasn't God. It was my own unrealistic expectations. As long as they were in place, I was never going to be enough in my own eyes.

God loves me even when I fall short. He loves me when I succeed. He loves me because I am His. It's been a long, hard lesson to learn, to believe deep in my soul that God made me unique and special. He made you that way too. No one else has the qualifications for the work He has planned for us. For me, it isn't journalism, and I'm at peace with that. I'm off the hook. I'm just His. Wife, mother, writer, or pastor's wife—it doesn't matter; God loves me because I'm His daughter, not for any role I have. He feels the same way about you. He loves you for being you.

We were created to be in relationship with Him first. Ignore that relationship, and things get shaky. Making time for God makes me a better person. I'm a better wife and mother because the Spirit flows through me. When our relationships are solid, our footing is grounded. When things happen, as they do in both family life and ministry, we don't get knocked around so easily if we're firmly planted. Temptation isn't so beguiling.

Personally, I'm much easier to be around if I've spent some time with God. Relationship is a two-way street. Taking some quiet time with God relieves me of the pressure of carrying around worries and anxieties. It helps me surrender what I want. It lets me know who is really in control. (Not me!) I can pour out my heart to a trustworthy friend and never have to worry about it getting around.

Letting go of control can be totally freeing. All the fears, anxieties, and worries work like chains, holding me down. When I release them into God's care, I am then free to do the work He wants me to do and to be the person He created me to be.

I work better beside my husband when I'm assured of my relationship with God. Our partnership is more cohesive. It's an ebb and flow. Friction, when it comes, is dealt with in a more positive manner. As we partner in ministry with our spouses or lead our own ministries, being on the same page as our spouses is a huge benefit. I really believe this is what God intended.

ROLES

God formed Eve out of Adam's rib, not from the ground. Everything else was formed from the dust of the earth. John MacArthur says this:

First, it speaks of Eve's fundamental equality with Adam. The woman was "taken out of man." They shared the same essential nature. She was not a different kind of creature; she was of exactly the same essence as Adam. She was in no way an inferior character made merely to serve him, but she was his spiritual counterpart, his intellectual coequal, and in every sense his perfect mate and companion.[4]

Eve was never meant to be subservient to Adam. She was created to be his partner. I love that MacArthur talks not just about the physical aspect of her created being but also about her being Adam's spiritual and intellectual counterpart. She met all of Adam's needs, and he met hers. As a couple, they were a whole. Complete. They complemented each other.

As wives in ministry, do we complement our husbands? Are we coequal? These are good questions to ask ourselves. *Collins English Dictionary* gives this meaning of the word *coequal:* "1. of the same size, rank, etc. 2. a person or thing equal with another."[5] We may have different jobs, but the reality is, we are equal. God did not create one better than the other. He created us different. To work together. To be pieces of a puzzle that fit together. We listen and support each other, talk things over.

Both my husband and I love to read. We get jazzed reading books about the Holy Spirit and church. We dream about what church could look like, and we work together to that end. I don't have a Bible degree, but that doesn't mean I can't or don't want to learn. As I read and study the Bible, guess what? Not only do I meet God and get to know Him better, but as a bonus I'm starting to understand my husband's job better and the call on his life, as well as on my own. Our relationship only benefits from this kind of interaction. It deepens it.

As spouses, we will each interpret the parts we play differently. There is absolutely nothing wrong with this. We are all uniquely gifted. We were never meant to be the same, cookie cutter images of each other. Roles shift as seasons change in our lives. Life is very fluid, I'm learning.

When my boys were teeny tiny, my role was at home about 90 percent of the time. As they have gotten older, I have a little leeway to do things I'm interested in. One rule remains: our home is meant to be a refuge for my husband, the boys, and me. It's the only way we all stay sane. If that refuge is ever threatened, I have to go back and evaluate priorities again.

Was it always this way? A long way from it. We had to learn hard lessons from the crazy times. It almost cost us our sanity. Life becomes increasingly hard if our home is in turmoil or chaos. It's just how we're wired. Home is our refuge away from the hustle and bustle of church and the many demands that come from ministry.

As I mentioned, this isn't the way it was at first. Martha Stewart, I am not. I'm one of those people who are organized in their mess! I wanted to be a journalist because I wanted adventure, not the mundane cleaning schedule that still eludes me. I didn't want to bake cookies every week or clean and mop and wipe. For me, this has been part of making a refuge, but it's not all of it.

A refuge for our family is a place where we all feel welcomed, loved, and accepted. Routine is also a part of a refuge, as we all thrive when a regular routine is in place. This is what works for my family in making a refuge to come home to when all else is chaos. Yours may look totally different. That's okay. It's better than okay.

As my boys grow, my role is changing. I have a little more freedom to pursue my desires and dreams. I'm still here for them when they come home from school, but it's different than when they were really small. Now they need me to be here so if stuff happens at school (and it does!) they can talk to me about it or at least know I'm here if they want to talk. They need me emotionally much more now.

My role is still Mom, but it's expanding. It also changed when my husband, after being an associate pastor for many years, became the senior pastor. Roles change because our husbands change roles!

I am testing my wings as I discover my new roles. I attend Bible studies, write, and seek what else God had in mind when He called me to ministry alongside my husband. Some days getting to this particular time felt like forever. Eventually it became a reality.

Maybe your work role is out in the marketplace, which brings many challenges to the role of pastor's wife. It's a lot of responsibility. I always say I have a part-time job already as a pastor's wife, so to work full time would be a job and a half! You have to figure out how to make it all work. Family, church, and work—wow! That's a lot to contend with. Most likely you are still expected, and hopefully desire, to fulfill some kind of ministry role. That's a job and a half.

Creativity is vital in organizing it all. Maybe it means saying no to a whole lot of extras and making your home and family number one. Everyone else gets a no right now. Maybe your church needs to see that no is a good word at times. Family is a good priority. Only you and God can figure out what's best for you and your family and your church. Ask Him; He longs to talk to you about it.

WORSHIP

As seasons fluctuate I have to be very intentional about keeping God, family, and then ministry as my priorities, in that order. It's so easy to get it reversed! I want to run ahead and do my own thing. I can get so involved with a project that I get tunnel vision. I don't want to deal with laundry and spills. I don't want to be a wife and mom today. I don't want to have coffee with someone from the church!

When God created Eve, He performed "a special act of creation."[6] The Lord said it was not good for Adam to be alone. So God provided what was good for Adam: Eve. Helper and companion. I like what *The Expositor's Bible Commentary* has to say about Genesis 2:18: "The implication of the narrative is that in both of these areas of life, the family and worship, man stands in need of the woman's help. It is not good that he should be alone."[7] They are meant to be a team. Sometimes, in our household, that means we take shifts! This is so one of us can pursue a dream for a while or take a badly needed break. It can mean that one of us gives the other a shove in the right direction. Perhaps from the rear!

Why is it important for us to take a break? To worship. I find in our house, worship can be a struggle. If you lead worship in church, in either music or teaching, services aren't always conducive to praise! I'm not saying it can't be, but some days it feels more like work than worship.

Who is *our* pastor? Who helps us meet our spiritual needs? These are questions we ask ourselves. Again, flexibility and creativity are key.

Our spouses need help with family and worship. Many times they get caught up in the day-to-day ministry, which involves everything from mini crises to major issues to life-or-death situations. They need a reminder to come back to real life—a kindly reminder sometimes, and a good kick other times. Being in leadership can be addictive, and part of my job is to keep my husband grounded. "Mark, the toilet needs fixing. The boys need some Daddy-time. We're still here." When we parent as a team, things go a lot smoother.

Corporate worship is another challenge. Mark needs time to worship elsewhere. He often downloads podcasts of other preachers he admires and listens to them when he's driving. It keeps him inspired and gets him out of his own church, even if it's by way of the Internet in the car. I'm so glad he does this, because for many years he wasn't being ministered to.

He follows some of those preachers on Twitter and there learns about new books he can read and blogs he can keep up with. We read a lot, as I mentioned before, and get fed that way too. Many of our mentors have been writers who have spoken into our lives through their books and words. At nighttime we listen to worship music and let the sounds soothe our household. I'm really glad that Mark studied worship and was a worship pastor first, as that has helped us broaden our horizons. Every day is an opportunity to see God and to show Him our praise and appreciation. Worship isn't just about Sunday morning. It can be while walking on a Monday evening or listening to worship music while we work or play with the kids. Worship can happen at any time of any day, which is great since it doesn't happen much on Sundays. Sunday in the pastor's household is a workday. You know it too. It's not really our Sabbath.

Our kids are young enough that it's still fun that Daddy is "the boss." After we moved to our current location, it wasn't so enjoyable. They struggled to adjust to a new, very different, church. They'd left behind the church they had grown up in, with all the bells and whistles, and came to one that is more traditional. It was hard for them. They sat in church for the opening worship, yawning and hanging their heads until they were released for Sunday school. I was a little concerned, as they used to be avid worshippers.

I sit midway in the congregation. I don't sit at the front with my husband, because I can't read the screens or watch videos if I sit so close. The boys had been sitting with me, but my husband decided to experiment and have them sit up front with him. The musicians and singers were closer, and it was much more interesting. It was a good call—they have livened up considerably! It took some teamwork to figure it out.

In both of these areas of family and worship, God knows what is good for us, what is best. We need each other. However, the enemy will do whatever he can to drive a wedge into the teamwork.

THE ENEMY

When I first started thinking about being called, I was very vain. I saw it as leading a public ministry. That's part of it, but not all of it. It may not be any of it. The calling is in the gritty, messy hard places. It's in all the things that happen behind the scenes. The private conversations between husbands and wives. Conflicts in marriages, including our own. Conflicts with other ministry leaders and members of the church or board. If people actually knew how much conflict there is in church, I think they would be shocked. Most of it is dealt with respectfully and quietly. Most of it.

Ministry is also in chatting over coffee with people who are growing in their relationship with Jesus and witnessing friends living out what they are learning. It can be rare, but it's so precious when it happens. The best ministry happens quietly. No public spectacle.

Part of the calling to ministry is to fight back, pushing back the enemy from our front doors. He lied to Eve in the garden; he'll lie to us too. His slick words cause us to question and doubt God and His motives. Eve was Satan's original victim. "Did God really say, 'You must not eat from any tree in the garden'?" (Genesis 3:1 NIV). He put doubt in Eve's ear. God said she couldn't eat from *one* tree, not from *any* tree. According to *The Expositor's Bible Commentary*, "The inference of God's commands in vv.16–17 is that God alone knows what is good…for man and that God alone knows what is not good…for him. To enjoy the 'good' man must trust God alone and obey him."[8] I enjoy the good that God has planned for me so much more if I'm obedient and trusting. I want the good so badly, but my earthly flesh battles me. The lies the enemy whispers become louder and make me question and doubt, opening the door—wide at times—to his cunning and causing friction and chaos. *I am no longer good. I am not good enough.*

The best way I know to fight back is to get low on our knees in prayer. Put on the armour. Take our thoughts captive, and refuse to hand the victory to Satan. The enemy wants us to give up because if we do, he wins. He's taken out a formidable soldier. You may not think you're good enough, but the truth is, you are good. You are a warrior that Satan doesn't want to deal with. That's what we are—soldiers in the kingdom army. *He* knows it. He doesn't want *you* to.

If Satan can tempt a pastor or other leader in the church to stumble, it's a big victory for him because it's not just the leader who falls. He or she usually takes a few followers down with him or her. When my husband and I are working together as a team, as a whole, it makes us impenetrable from the outside. The enemy can't get in. When we aren't, it's a disaster waiting to happen! That wedge between us gives Satan a foot in the door. He's the kind that if given an inch will take a mile. We don't want to open that door a sliver!

Fighting my calling or my husband's calling wears me down and drains my marriage and everything else of joy. It takes all my energy to fight it. I've watched as my friends have given up. Marriages ended because someone just couldn't fight it anymore. I wonder if they thought they found something better. A better husband or wife. A better life. Maybe they couldn't reconcile themselves to a life in ministry. The battle drained the very life out of them. It ran like blood out of a vein. They walked away because they couldn't walk forward into it anymore.

Is it worth the fight? Against God? Against your husband? I'm not so sure. I've raged in that battle. When I stopped, life was so much more peaceful. I was afraid that accepting the truth and stopping the fighting would make me a doormat. It didn't. I'm not a doormat—I'm a warrior.

I am stronger. My energy isn't spent fighting something that isn't going to change. Instead I'm channelling it into a far greater purpose. I'm doing it on both my and God's terms. No one else's. This has been part of my journey—learning how to be a pastor's wife and accept my calling but in a way that both honours God and is true to myself. It's about my relationship with God and who I am in Him. Not some role I play. The world doesn't need more masks, more role-playing. People are looking for authentic leaders who live out what they teach. How they lead is how they live. This is what I'm starting to understand as my calling.

It means accepting myself as I am. Yes, change needs to happen. The old, withered, and dead stuff really does need to be removed. It's painful. But in the pain is regrowth. Maturity. Other things, like personality and interests, are there for a reason. Can I accept them? Can I use them for God and His kingdom? It's something to think about and explore.

I'm learning that God wants me to be a woman of influence. For Him. This role of being married to the pastor doesn't have to be a bad thing! I can use it to point others to Jesus. If I am true to who God created me to be and I live with authenticity and honesty, then there are no limits. God can do anything! He is our hope. If, as a pastor's wife, I can influence people for Jesus and point them to Him, then I'm okay with that role, that title.

One last thing about Eve: she was redeemed. She made a mess—a colossal mess—not just for herself and Adam *but for all humanity!* Yet God redeemed her and used her to start the human race. Life was hard after the garden, but it was still worth it. It set in motion God's plan for salvation.

We aren't perfect either. We make messes. Sometimes huge ones! Maybe you already have made such a bad mess that you think there's no hope for you—especially as a pastor's wife. Let me reassure you: God redeemed Eve, and He will you, too. Just ask.

God has used some of my biggest messes and pains to bring me closer to Him. He's used them to make me more accessible to the women I serve because I was honest about my life and my mistakes. The women in your congregation don't need a perfect spiritual saint; they need a friend to walk the journey with them, sharing lessons and laughter and tears. Eventually it will all lead back to Eden, only this time Eden will be not a garden but heaven itself.

Chapter Two

Desperate

The questions haunted me: *What if the leadership of the church finds out about my problem? What if my husband loses his job because of me? Why can't I control this insidious anger? How many times will I scream and yell at my children, at my husband? What will it take for me to stop?*

My heart was sick and broken. Like Paul, I did what I did not want to do (Romans 7:16). But was that really true? Did I really want to stop? Anger is a choice, and I kept choosing it. I was not like Paul at all. I was a fraud, and I was going to be found out.

Anger had been brewing deep down within me for some time. Normally I was able to keep a lid on it, but occasionally something, like criticism, would trigger it. I would freak if anyone said anything critical, constructive or not. I would stew about it and then have a total meltdown at home. Because I had to keep up appearances.

My anger was no longer contained. As a new mom totally overwhelmed by a baby and a two-year-old who didn't sleep much and ran like a cheetah for the better part of the day, I was coming to the end of my rope. It was becoming a serious issue. Having a busy husband who worked overtime didn't help. The church was short-staffed, so Mark had taken on extra duties in the worship department. Although he was no longer a worship pastor, when that role became vacant they needed his experience. So he was doing two people's jobs in a busy church.

The new job had come with a move to a new city in another province. Moving across the country is never easy. Leaving the slow pace of New Brunswick for the driven pace of Ontario resulted in culture shock. We'd lived in the Maritimes for just over two years, but we had adapted to the slower pace quite nicely. It took some getting used to—being back in Ontario, in a busy, busy church of one thousand people.

When we arrived in our new city, I was eight months pregnant with our second child. My husband had closed our dying church in New Brunswick and then was unemployed for five months. We lived with my parents while my husband interviewed with churches. He got a job and commuted for a couple of months. We bought a house, and two months later my toddler and I joined him in the new city.

Life got busier, and I got angrier. With the birth of a second beautiful baby boy, life should have been good. But I was seething. I screamed and yelled at my babies. I hated the monster I was becoming. I couldn't control the anger that kept coming from nowhere. It had totally mastered me. On top of that, I was severely sleep deprived. My toddler always woke up the baby from his nap, and they would never sleep at the same time. My toddler had not slept much since infancy, so I was already tired by the time baby number two came along. I couldn't get a break, and it was breaking me.

I was alone with the kiddos all day and many nights as my husband worked. I felt like a single mom. Resentment started to build at my husband's absence. It was like rubbing salt in an already festering wound, so I yelled at him too.

It got so I was afraid to get out of bed in the morning. Afraid of how and when I was going to blow it that day. Afraid I was going to hurt someone. Sure of failure. These were no longer bad moods or a bad day. *Every day was a bad day.* Every new day mocked me, and fear fuelled the anger. I just wanted to cover my head and disappear.

In an odd sort of irony, I wanted to be invisible, but part of the problem was that I already felt invisible. I had no help. No support system. No parents or in-laws close by to come over or let me get some sleep. We were so new to the area that I didn't know the women who had offered to look after the boys well enough to let them, and I was too new a mom to trust anyone. Again fear kept me in a self-imposed prison. I spent most days at home with the boys, invisible to the outside world. At church I was too busy with the boys to really get to know many people. There wasn't time to talk to anyone between getting the kiddos from the nursery and Sunday school. I was alone, overwhelmed, and frustrated. I felt angry all the time. I was trying to survive and get everyone out alive.

I was alone because I kept all of this a secret. I was desperately afraid: afraid someone would take my kids away. Afraid of being found out. Afraid of what could happen if I wasn't found out! Afraid for my family. I didn't think an angry, sometimes abusive, pastor's wife would go over too well. I didn't want my husband to lose his job because of me. I thought of the shame, humiliation, and gossip should that happen. And so the secrets, the loneliness, and the fear kept growing. They were about to swallow me whole. I just needed someone…who would listen, who would not judge, who would not cast me aside. I was desperate.

I just needed someone…who would listen, who would not judge, who would not cast me aside. I was desperate.

DESPERATE HOPE

She was an outcast, considered unclean. She had been cast out of society, both emotionally and physically. Thrown out with the trash. She was cut off from everyone and everything she loved. Alone. Perhaps fearful. Or maybe she had gotten used to the fear. By now it was more of a nagging sore that she ignored.

The bleeding was chronic. She had tried everything and gone to anyone who would try to heal her, who would give her hope. She was desperate.

The Gospel of Mark tells the story of this woman, who touched the robe of Jesus to be healed from her chronic bleeding. It's a story about desperate hope—desperate hope for healing from disease, loneliness, and alienation.

Jesus was on His way to heal the dying daughter of Jarius, a synagogue ruler. People crowded around Him. Because the bleeding woman was an outcast, she was not supposed to approach Jesus—or any other person. She was unclean. She had been suffering with this disease for twelve years. As the Gospel of Mark records it, she had been "subject to bleeding for twelve years" (Mark 5:25). The bleeding had mastered her, and she was its subject. "She was ashamed of her ceremonial 'uncleanness'...caused by a disease which cut her off from everything. According to the law such a sufferer infected everything she touched with her uncleanliness. She was absolutely shut off from the worship of God and the fellowship of other men and women."[9] Shunned, she was no longer a part of civilized society. Talk about loneliness! She was unacceptable. Unclean. Rejected. Abandoned. Cast aside.

She had tried as many cures as doctors, but she grew worse, not better. Finally, she heard about Jesus and turned to Him for healing (Mark 5:26–27). He was her only hope if she was ever going to return to society, family, and friends. If she was ever going to become visible again.

I wonder what took her so long to seek out Christ. Maybe she hadn't heard about Him before, although I would think that those who were sick and cast off probably knew about Jesus and His healing power. Maybe she couldn't get to Him because she wasn't supposed to be among the clean. She was afraid to try at first. Maybe she thought she wasn't good enough to seek Jesus out, to ask for something like healing. Then a nagging in the back of my mind clarifies itself: why does it take me so long to seek out Christ?

PHYSICIANS OF NO VALUE

"It is usual with people not to apply themselves to Christ, till they have tried in vain all other helpers, and find them, as certainly they will, *physicians of no value*."[10] *Physicians of no value.* How many times have I sought out physicians of no value instead of Christ?

Let me name a few. The physician of consumerism—after I would have an angry fit, I would sometimes leave the house when Mark got home. It's a good thing to take some time, a moment. But instead of going to be by myself and pray, I would go to a toy store. I'd buy a few things for the boys. In denial, I would think I was helping myself, that having a few things on hand to do with the boys would prevent me from getting angry. In reality I was trying to buy their love and acceptance and smooth over my very rough edges.

Then there was the physician of blame—blaming anyone or anything but myself. I was tired. I was alone a lot. I had some legitimate excuses. But did I really? Nothing excuses bad behaviour. I had to own up to my problem and take responsibility, but I couldn't do that on my own. And I couldn't do it while visiting a physician of no value. I needed the one true healer.

Other physicians of no value are food, alcohol, shoes, gambling, or work. We visit one doctor, but the problem can't be solved, so we go to another one and another one. But deep down we know what the real problem is, don't we? We're looking in the wrong places for answers. We are seeking out bandages when what we really need is a diagnosis.

A question popped into my head: Could it also be that we don't seek out God because we feel separated or abandoned by Him? I was ashamed of my behaviour. When I lost my temper, I always felt a physical separation from God. I would feel numb, incapable of any kind of emotional engagement, like there was a gaping void right in the centre of my soul. God hadn't moved; I had. I hid in shame. I hid in regret. I hid in sorrow. I hid in denial. I didn't want to go there, to the throne of grace, because I didn't like what I was going to see—the mess of me. Then I'd have to face the consequences for all of us, my whole family. None of us were unscathed. I didn't want to deal with it. I didn't think I had the strength.

It's a lonely place, that space of finding out that your physicians of no value are really that—of no value. That sin has come between you and God.

On top of the anger, there was the loneliness of being a pastor's wife. It didn't help matters. As I said, I felt that I really couldn't get honest with others about my problems.

I know that many pastors' wives experience this intense loneliness and fear. I hear it in conversations; I read about it in blogs and articles. We feel unloved—by God, by our husbands, and by the churches we serve. We have sacrificed our gifts and families so our husbands can be free to go and do what they were called to do. We stay home for the season of little ones and babies. We see our husbands adored and thanked while our family's sacrifices go unnoticed. It's hurtful because we've given up so much to free up our husbands. Gifts and talents are put on hold. It feels like our calls to ministry have evaporated or died as our time is taken up with children and parenting. Being a good mom is a very special calling and is worth the sacrifice. I'm not saying it isn't. However, there are times when we ache to fulfill our other calling. We forget in the moment that it's temporary. It's a "Wait" not a "Dead End" sign.

It's hard to see others doing what we want to do. Even harder when we're trying to get away from what we were called to do. When we haven't accepted our calling or our husband's, turmoil and pain come calling. We're fighting not only our husband but God and the entire church. All these things cause us to become separated from our heavenly Father, and there is great loneliness in that. We are shut off from Him and others. We feel like an outcast in our own church or a trophy that no one really cares about. The fear and the secrets keep us invisible.

We don't always want to be seen. We run from God rather than seek Him out first—until there is no other place to turn. No more physicians to offer false hope. No more places to hide. Just desperation, a desperate hope in one person.

> *When she heard about Jesus, she came up behind him in the crowd and touched his cloak, because she thought, "If I just touch his clothes, I will be healed." Immediately her bleeding stopped and she felt in her body that she was freed from her suffering.* (Mark 5:27–29)

This woman recognized the real thing when she saw it. She knew she wouldn't be allowed to speak to Jesus because of her uncleanness, but that didn't stop her. She believed that all she had to do was touch His clothing, and she would be healed. Just a little of Jesus would be enough. She had tremendous faith, fuelled by desperate hope.

HEALING

She received healing by touching his cloak. But a little of Jesus is never enough.

> The excitement of the miracle story about the woman with the issue of blood is extraordinary and beautiful. It is as though time stood still. Amid the thronging and jostling of the crowd, Jesus stopped. For the moment only the woman and her need existed. In a day and age when the individual tends to get lost in the crowd it is especially significant that to God one person is never like another; each is individual, with all God's love and power at his disposal.[11]

He asked, "Who touched my clothes?" (Mark 5:30). He calls us out. Isn't that what we're looking for? Don't you feel like you get lost in the crowd of needy parishioners? That what *you need* is often overlooked?

I've often asked, *Who is my pastor?* Just for one moment, I want me and my need to be the only things that exists. To know that God knows me, that He's asking for me. "Who touched my clothes?"

Jesus ignored His disciples' comments that it was ridiculous to think someone in the crowd touched Him purposefully. It would have been like being at a U2 concert—people crushing in on all sides. Claustrophobic. No room to breathe. Verse 32 says, "But Jesus kept looking around to see who had done it." He was on his way to heal a young girl *who was dying*, but that didn't stop him from helping this woman. He wasn't in a hurry. He knew who touched Him. He wasn't going to let her get away. He knew what else she needed: Complete healing. Healing of infirmities. Healing of insecurities. Healing of feelings of worthlessness. It's what we all need. Healing of feelings of not making the grade. Healing of our resentment and anger. Healing of our unforgiveness. A little of Jesus is just not enough. He always works in abundant measures. He sees our hearts.

Jesus singled out this woman, not to punish her but to encourage her.[12] She saw Him, face to face. She wasn't an outcast to Jesus. That must have meant the world to this woman. He wanted to know who touched Him. Not for Himself, but for her. Not to demean her, but to give her life.

This is amazing! It makes my heart beat faster. Jesus singled out a woman who had been thrown away by society, not to condemn her but to encourage her and bring glory to His Father. The God of Creation reached down and healed her and also gave her back her dignity in front of a thronging crowd—a crowd she wasn't even supposed to be in, because of her uncleanliness! How just like Jesus!

He calls us out. Not to condemn. Although we deserve condemnation, God gives us grace. He calls us out into the light so that our dark places can be exposed and we can experience healing, just like the woman who bled.

I had to own up to my sins—my rage, my resentment, my bitterness and unforgiveness. But God is gentle, and He deals with each of us in a way that touches our hearts, if we let Him. He wants to heal our hearts.

I went for counselling for my anger issues from a godly Christian woman who affected me in life-changing ways. *One grace.* At the same time, I was asked to work on the choreography for our Christmas production. *Two graces.* And then I was asked to dance in the production. *Three graces.* I had never done any kind of choreography in a church setting, and it would be the first time I danced at the church.

For me, dancing has always been peaceful. No matter what else was going on, I could go to my dance class and lose myself in that one hour. I wouldn't be afraid. I wouldn't worry. It was safe, and I was in a world all my own. So doing the choreography, as well as dancing myself, was very cathartic. Combined with the counselling, that time was a great source of healing. But God went even farther. He called me out.

I was quite nervous about dancing. At our dress rehearsal, our pastor spoke to the cast and reminded us that what really mattered was our audience of one. I felt calmed by that. It only mattered that God was there. And I took it one step further. Could I also just dance with God? He and I? I thought I could. And so that weekend, I had an audience of one and a wonderful dance partner. God came down and met me on that stage while I danced. I felt His favour. It was like a warm glow washing over me. Like a light flowing over and with me.

I could see the audience, a few familiar faces. It didn't throw me off my dance. It only added to the experience, because I knew my friends were seeing a part of me that they had never seen before, that few people in my life had ever seen before.

I felt His grace. I knew I was a sinner, but I felt forgiven. His grace was like a veil covering me. I felt hope. He is always a God of abundance. He didn't focus on my bad behaviour—I had done enough of that. I knew I was wrong. And He knew too. He looked at my heart. It was sick, but He could see it whole again.

We see only the here and now, the mess we've made. God looks at the heart, as it says in 1 Samuel 16:7. He doesn't look at outward appearances. He sees the women He created us to be, not the works in progress that we are.

Don't we do just the opposite? We see and imagine the worst. At least I do. I remember when my son acted out, I'd worry about what he'd be like in fifteen years. My therapist told me that I had to stop thinking that way. To see him *now*. That's what God sees, the here and now, but He also sees what we can become in the future. He doesn't multiply our transgressions fifteen times; rather, He multiplies our good fifteen times and more. He extends grace and love.

I felt loved that weekend I danced. It was the beginning of healing. He called me out of the crowd, out of hiding, and dealt with me and my heart in a way that was special and meaningful for me. He knows me because He created me. He knows that dancing speaks to my soul and that it can heal me like nothing else. Like when He brought the woman out of the crowd to make her whole, He does the same with us.

"Daughter, your faith has healed you. Go in peace and be freed from your suffering" (Mark 5:34). Jesus calls her "daughter" and in one fell swoop brings her back into acceptable society. But He also brings her into His heavenly family by acknowledging her as a daughter of the King. He validates her faith. And He blesses her. *Go in peace and be freed from your suffering.* He knew what she had suffered. He understands our suffering. Sometimes our pain is caused by our own poor choices. Other times, we suffer because of others' poor choices.

If we're honest about our struggles and deal with them, then peace can come and reside within us. We can be set free from those chains that imprison us. *Then* He can take those scars, those cast-off chains, and use them to bring glory to His Father in heaven. We can hold them up and say "Look! Once I was a prisoner; now I am free!"

I have been open and honest about my struggle with anger for a number of years now. God has taken that and used it to help others. Women have told me their stories or just whispered, "I was an angry mom too!" The relief of just admitting that is tangible. It's the first step to healing. We don't have to hide behind our dirty little secret, in fear and shame. That's why Jesus came and died on the cross for us, so the fear and shame would be put to death. Our sin is no longer an issue, because He conquered it. He loves us that much!

He can take your struggle, whatever it is, and use it too. There is someone out there who needs to hear your story of hope and redemption. Of Jesus. If the physicians of no value that you've been seeking out aren't working for you, turn to Jesus. Others may have cast you aside, and you may feel washed out or no good. He doesn't see you like that. He sees the real you. He sees your heart. He's ready, to help and heal, whenever you are. Don't wait. Seek His face. He is the one true physician.

Chapter Three

Warrior

I love watching a good sword fight. Maybe it's because I love my boys, and sword fights are a part of their DNA. We've watched plenty of movies where the hero and villian wielded swords or light sabres, which are really high-tech swords! They engage my imagination.

To use swords well, you have to be fleet footed and extremely coordinated. A good strategist. Strong. Swords are heavy. The idea of being a warrior in God's military sends chills up my spine. It ignites the fighting spirit in me. It does something else too. It puts to death the myth of what a pastor's wife should look like.

What's your idea of a pastor's wife, what she should be and do? We all have an idea. It may be hidden deep, or it may be something we aspire to because we've had a good role model.

Stereotypes of pastors' wives make me cringe. The piano-playing, choir-singing wife. The perfectly coifed wife who seems to have it all together. The meek and mild wallflower. The super saint. There's more, but these ones in particular are my thorns. They poke at me. In a twisted way, they make me more insecure, while at the same time I want to run as far away from them as possible.

It's the stereotypes I can't stand, not the actual women. They become larger than life in my mind. I struggle with the super saint and the wallflower. One is too saintly. She's no good to anyone, a woman no one can relate to. Unapproachable.

The wallflower scares me. Don't put that persona on me! I don't want to be seen as a doormat. Uninspiring. Over the years, I've rebelled more against this one because I knew I could easily *be* her. I like parking up against the wall, especially in new situations. Introverted, I like being alone for long stretches, to read, write, and reflect. To rejuvenate. The foyer of a church is my living nightmare. People want to chitchat. I'm usually in a hurry, running after the boys. I don't hear well in noisy places. I have to get people to repeat what they've said at least two times. Or I pretend I heard them and smile and nod. This can get awkward if I'm not supposed to be smiling or nodding. I'm not at my finest in the church foyer. I often feel like there's a neon light flashing around me, screaming out that I'm a mess. A misfit. So the idea of sidling up to a wall and not making a sound is quite appealing.

At the same time, I have noticed a few spouses who remind me of those stereotypes. I self-righteously think, *Don't hide; live your life. You've got much influence here on planet Earth, so use it for God's glory.* Have I bought into that stereotype? Have I prejudged her? Labelled her? Yes, I have. It's so easy to fall into those thought patterns, into judgment. Even for those of us who are fighting those images!

Nobody wants to see herself in any kind of stereotype, even if it's a good one. We want to be unique.

Nobody wants to see herself in any kind of stereotype, even if it's a good one. We want to be unique. One of my chief struggles being married to a pastor has been my internal battle against the image of a pastor's wife. I wondered if accepting the invitation to be a fisher of people would cram me into a mould I would never fit in. I worried that if I started to take my role as a pastor's wife seriously, I might become one of them. That's why the idea of a warrior's heart appeals to me. Inspires me! It takes the victimization out of ministry and brings back the sense of purpose, why we're doing this in the first place.

Purpose keeps us focused in the throes of battle. My own experience of ministry with my husband has been fairly bloody on some occasions. Mark's first full-time position as a worship pastor started out well enough. Things looked okay on the surface. We quickly discovered that things are not always what they appear to be. "Okay" was a lie. Things were definitely *not* okay. There were some cracks in the congregation and leadership. They deepened into fissures and then open chasms. The church imploded. The fallout was deadly.

From our perspective, years of turmoil had fuelled the smouldering hidden fire. The hiring of Mark seemed to be the breaking point for this fragile congregation, the catalyst for a gut-wrenching church fight. Fingers were pointed at the leadership. The church took sides and split. After two years, the full-time staff had been reduced to one—my husband.

Honestly, we were only there because we had no other place to go. Meetings almost ended in fisticuffs. Fragmented friendships and families lay scattered like war casualties. People left because they couldn't reconcile what was happening. How could people who say they love Jesus act this way? Satan had a field day. He does every time a church fights inside its walls.

It's something we in polite church society don't like to talk about *ever*, but certainly not in public. *We should*. Over half of my husband's twenty years in pastoral experience have been spent dealing with church conflict.

Leaders come in all shapes and sizes, each with their own set of special skills and gifts. Some deal with conflict well, and others do not. It's a learned skill. Forged. I came to think of my husband as God's janitor. He was very good at cleaning up messes. After you navigate successfully through a maelstrom, others want you on their team.

Ministry isn't for the faint-hearted. It's not a matter of *if* conflict will occur; it's *when*. Everyone is going to deal with trouble and trials at some point in ministry. Like many of you, we've experienced our fair share of crises and conflicts. Maybe that's why God instills us with a warrior's heart. He knows that a pastor's wife needs to be able to fight by her husband's side and at times for him. She has to fight for her family. She has to fight for herself, for the local church, and for those she loves in the church, in the community. So God graciously gives many of us the heart of a fighter.

SURRENDER

There's a woman in the Bible who had such a heart. Deborah's mentioned in the book of Judges, chapter 4. It's just a snapshot of a period in her life. She was a judge, a mediator, settling disputes among the Israelites. A prophet whose voice was respected in a male-dominated society. A woman whose love of God and willingness to follow Him to the ends of the earth, even to war, surmounted all barriers and boundaries. Her heart was that of a soldier.

A warrior's heart must be tamed, or else it can get out of control. It's got to learn to surrender. Sounds like an oxymoron, right? A surrendered soldier. But it's not an oxymoron at all. Look at the training involved in becoming good soldiers. They learn to obey their leader no matter what. They learn to trust their commander and each other. They are bonded together by surrendering their own rights and desires. They are committed to their team and their country, willing to sacrifice themselves for them.

Beyond Deborah's successful exterior as a judge was a woman deeply committed to God and her people. Her life was surrendered to God's will. She was willing to do whatever God desired.

Deborah was the fourth judge of Israel, the only woman. She was also a prophetess. Matthew Henry says Deborah was "entirely devoted to the service of Israel. She judged Israel at the time that Jabin oppressed them...She judged, not as a princess, by any civil authority conferred upon her, but as a prophetess, and as God's mouth to them."[13] In other words, she was put in her job by God, to do His will.

Deborah, I imagine, at some point must have had a conversation with God. I'm thinking it went something like this: "How is this going to work? I'm a woman. I'm not qualified for this position. The men are not going to take me seriously, let alone listen to me! What are You thinking, Lord? I don't fit in here!"

Then, later, "Okay, I'll do it." In those four words, she surrendered to the plan that God had for her life, which would have been so different from what she grew up thinking she'd be! It must have been hard. I'm sure she wrestled with it, but in the end she let go of her desires and plans and followed God. Once she did, her whole life was contrary to everything the world said.

Surrendering our will to God makes us as Christians unique. Our lives are no longer about what the world says is important: success, money, fame, me first. We are called to be different. I have sat countless times thinking, *I don't fit in here! This is so not what I thought I'd be doing!* I wanted a career, money, recognition. A servant leader? Come on! A stay-at-home mom? No way! Boring! It hasn't been at all like I thought—or planned. I've had that conversation: "Lord, how is this going to work? I'm not qualified for this position. We don't have the money for me to stay at home. What were You thinking, Lord? I don't fit in here!" It was exhausting because *I was fighting the wrong enemy.* I needed to learn to let go and trust God. To believe that I was exactly the person He wanted in this exact place. If I believe that, then I'm ready to obey Him, which also sets me up to be ready to fight the enemy.

I was constantly angry and frustrated; nothing made me happy. The words "Okay, I'll do it" have not come easily. They've taken a ridiculously long time. Some days I repeat them over and over because I've taken back control. "Okay, I'll stay home. Okay, I'll let this dream sit a while longer. Okay, I'll love, even though some days I don't feel like it. Okay, I'll pour myself into this life. Okay, I'll make our house into a home. Okay, I'll do it, even though I'm afraid."

What have I learned from this daily laying down of my wants, my rights, my life? I've realized how much I want to control everything about my life, and I've learned to let go of the control I'm so desperate to have. Letting God be in charge is scary. I don't know what's going to happen. I like to know the agenda. Letting go means I have to trust.

It's easy when I know what's coming next: home, soccer, dinner, homework, bedtime. I love routine. When it's chaotic or questionable, fear rises. Can I trust God if people are pointing their fingers at my husband because they don't like his decisions? Can I trust God if half the church leaves? Can I trust God if lies are told about me or my family? If my kids are criticized?

Did Deborah feel that way? If she did, she didn't let it stop her from trusting God and obeying Him. She gave up her own plans for her life and trusted God with what He wanted to do.

When I trust God, obedience comes much easier. If I don't trust God, obedience will never happen! If my children trust my judgment because I've made sound decisions, they are more likely to obey me. I've proven myself trustworthy. It's the same with God. I have to trust Him in order to become the pastor's wife I want to be. I have to trust that in accepting His call I won't become one of those stereotypes.

At first it was hard. I'd panic and push back against it. *I am not that!* The battle to have my own way would start. My mood would turn combative. There was no way I was going to co-operate with either God or Mark. Like a little petulant child, I would clench my fists and say those words every parents hates: *You can't make me!* My ears and heart were shut tight to His gentle call. I had built walls so high, I didn't even realize that there were many parts of my life that still needed surrendering, especially the fight against being a pastor's wife. Like I've already mentioned, I was afraid it would define me. As long as I was in this tug of war with God, it would supersede everything else. Everyone was suffering, which I didn't want to happen. What I didn't realize was that I was the one suffering the most.

It was the wrong battle to fight. God gently whispered, "Stop. Let it go. You don't have to be this or that." Finally His voice penetrated my fear. I understood that He makes good things—me included. "For you created my inmost being; you knit me together in my mother's womb. I praise you because I am fearfully and wonderfully made; your works are wonderful, I know that full well" (Psalm 139:13–14).

God planned for me to marry Mark, even though I have told Him many times that He made a mistake. You may have had the same conversation with God. He chose you to be your husband's partner. God wasn't wrong. You have special qualities that He's equipped you with to fulfill your calling. God takes our messes, our mistakes, and redeems them. He uses them to bring Himself glory.

We don't need to be someone else. God will use us as we are. He has a plan. If we can trust, then we don't need to be a copy of someone else…or a stereotype.

After surrendering this to God, I needed a shift in perspective, to look at the bigger picture. Surrendering didn't mean I couldn't be a warrior too. Relief flooded me.

I find Deborah inspiring because she was ready to do battle. Heart and head ready! She was committed to God and what He told her to do. It wasn't an easy command, either. She was to go and confront Barack, the head of the military, and tell him what to do. Really? A woman going to tell the head of the army what the battle plan is going to be! Do you think that thrilled Deborah?

Barack seemed a little thick-headed. He put his trust in Deborah instead of God. He wanted her on the battlefield, like she was some sort of talisman. God obviously was not happy with Barack's lack of trust in Him. God had Deborah tell Barack that he wouldn't get the glory for the victory. A woman would. Can you imagine having to go and tell the military commander such a thing? I'm sure it left a bad taste in Deborah's mouth, but she trusted God and did the hard thing.

She accompanied Barack and his soldiers to the battlefield. The Canaanites had nine hundred iron chariots. As Gary Inrig says, "Those iron chariots represented state-of-the-art military technology."[14] The Israelites were up against a giant. Like any military operation, this was going to be dangerous. It seemed impossible that the outcome could be anything but a loss for the Israelites. Deborah jumped right in when necessary and did what needed to be done. If Deborah was afraid, Scripture doesn't tell us. She did what was asked of her. She was no wallflower.

Although most of us do not have real military battles to deal with, we still have a kingdom to fight for. It may be in our churches or in our families, but it's definitely in the spiritual kingdom. The apostle Peter said this:

> *Be alert and of sober mind. Your enemy the devil prowls around like*
> *a roaring lion looking for someone to devour. Resist him, standing*
> *firm in the faith, because you know that the family of believers*
> *throughout the world is undergoing the same kind of sufferings.*
> *And the God of all grace, who called you to his eternal glory in*

Christ, after you have suffered a little while, will himself restore you and make you strong, firm and steadfast. To him be the power for ever and ever. (1 Peter 5:8–11)

Our enemy doesn't want the church to succeed. He'll go after anyone who is committed to Christ and the church. As pastoral families, we are on the front lines of battle whether we want to be or not. Whatever we think about our roles, Satan doesn't care. He'll use it against us. He has us and our loved ones in his crosshairs. We don't even have to guess at it. Bringing down a church starts with walking through the front doors of the parsonage or whatever house, hut, or apartment we live in.

As I write this, a church in a nearby city is mourning the loss of its senior pastor. He suffered with depression. He committed suicide, and he left behind many people who loved him. I don't even pretend to understand. The only thing I do understand is that this battle is real and the stakes are high.

We've all heard the horror stories. Abandonment. Rebellion. I know spouses who have struggled with depression and anger, including myself. Children walk away from the church, from God. It starts with the littlest things.

Saturdays have been notoriously bad days in our house. How about yours? Sickness comes knocking on Saturday nights. Nightmares too. Insomnia. Sleep deprivation is a cruel weapon. We wake up feeling terrible. For some of us, the last thing we want to do is go to church. All we want to do is pull the covers over our heads and stay in bed.

When the boys were small, my husband left early for church on Sunday mornings. I was left to get the three of us ready to go to church. I was tired and resentful. By the time we got to church, I was exhausted, sweating profusely, and had already yelled so much that I felt guilty just walking into the building. I could scoff or make excuses, tell myself it's not spiritual warfare. That's a lie. The bull's eye sits on everyone who follows Christ; no one is exempt. For those of us in ministry, those circles of black and red are a little bit bigger and brighter. I believe it. I've experienced it.

Everyone experiences turmoil at home and then has to go to church. For pastors' wives, it can cut a little deeper. Guilt and shame make us feel like frauds. *I'm supposed to be a leader, and here I am yelling at the kids and fighting with my husband as he's leaving to go preach God's message! Hypocrite!* This useless guilt can cause strife in the home. Our husbands can get distracted.

I'm not saying that a pastor's family shouldn't be a priority. Home needs his full attention. It's part of being a husband and father. However, our enemy uses needless strife as a distraction. He can't focus on his job. Or he uses his job as an excuse to get away from the strife. Our children see what happens at home, and if it's not in line with what we are telling them about God, they will question His legitimacy. His love. Do you see how Satan uses it all to fragment the family?

"For our struggle is not against flesh and blood, but against the rulers, against the authorities, against the powers of this dark world and against the spiritual forces of evil in the heavenly realms" (Ephesians 6:12). There's a battle going on, even if we can't see it or won't acknowledge it. I'd rather stand firm and alert than be caught off guard because I was ignorant or in denial. Too often I stand by afraid or too tired to care. God has already won the victory for us through Christ dying on the cross! He defeated Satan. Why don't we remember that? Why do we go around in defeat, thinking that things will never change? That we will never change?

This defeatist attitude has gripped me tightly. Why do we so readily believe the lie of Satan that we'll never win instead of the truth that Christ has already won it for us? Satan knows our weak points, and he goes after them. It's not something to dismiss or take lightly.

God is trustworthy, and Deborah knew this. Do I know this deep down? Staying in His Word, remembering His faithfulness, talking to Him, and remembering His presence all day are some of the tactics we can use every day in this battle to trust God and to protect ourselves and our families. Putting on the armour of God is a good preventive measure so we can stand our ground against the enemy in both big and small battles. Maybe the better way to view battles is as private and public. Some of our inner turmoil can be the most destructive privately. The big battles in the church that are public and messy are also deadly. The armour works in all situations.

The belt of truth and the breastplate of righteousness. The boots of peace: the church really needs those! Pick up that shield of faith and the helmet of salvation. Wield that sword of the Spirit! So we can stand our ground, and when it's all over, we are still standing! Pray always in the Spirit. We have to believe the battle is real if we are going to be prepared.

I want to be standing after the battle, but so many times I am not. I didn't recognize the enemy prowling around. I didn't protect myself or my loved ones. I got taken out at the knees when instead I should have been *on* my knees. I let resentment rule my mind and spirit along with anger and fear. I tried to go it on my own. I still do. I have to continuously surrender my will, my dreams, back to God.

Keeping a surrendered heart and an obedient spirit means we are slinging arrows at the enemy and deflecting his. He can't touch us if we are in God's will, if we are in step with Him and talking to him all day.

I am learning to cover my family in prayer. I'm a little slow to catch on sometimes! My husband switched jobs at one point, and it required us to move to a new city. Our young boys knew only one home, and this would be a big change for them. I knew there might be some bumps in the road for everyone, but because *we* were following God's calling, I naively didn't expect our children to suffer.

We moved in January, which meant mid-school year. We left an excellent school, only to be disappointed with the new one. The boys were bored in their new classes. The other students, who were also our neighbours, were well schooled in sex, horror movies, and foul language. It felt like the boys lost their innocence overnight. We were all mourning the loss that comes with moving. It took a long time to grieve, and it was a challenge for both my husband and me. These were real-life lessons for all of us. Our new place provided great teaching moments, but at the time, I wouldn't have chosen them.

All the change and unfamiliarity are forcing me to grow in trust and prayer. Again, it's about letting go of control. I can't always be with my boys, but God is. He sees. He has a plan, and I have to trust it. I can pray and fight against the evil one that way. God expects me to be ready and alert. My family depends on it. It isn't easy. Doing battle never is.

"'For I know the plans I have for you,' declares the LORD, 'plans to prosper you and not to harm you, plans to give you hope and a future. Then you will call on me and come and pray to me, and I will listen to you'" (Jeremiah 29:11–12). God was asking the Israelites to come back to Him. He wanted to give them hope and a future. He had good things for them. He wanted them to call to Him, and He would listen! Deborah was listening for God. Her heart was open and willing.

God is waiting for us to call out to Him so He can listen to us. Can we loosen our grips on our dreams, our plans, and trust Him with our lives? He has good things planned for us and our families: a hope and a future, even amid our circumstances. Surrender, obedience, and trust are the heart of a warrior.

Chapter Four

Waiting

Some days the wait is more than I can bear. Sometimes a wait feels more like a weight! It's crushing in on all sides. Everywhere, there it is. It can just about sink me.

Mark and I waited almost ten years to have children. Part of that wait was due to the fact that he was in seminary and we were barely getting by, just the two of us. Starting a family was not a priority for us those first few years.

I wasn't ready to be a mom, either. I was still trying to find my career, as I've explained in previous chapters. Nor am I a "kid person." Today I love my own boys, but I'm not the mom who wants to have a million kids over for playdates. It stresses me out. So Mark and I waited to have children until we wanted them.

Around my thirtieth birthday, we decided that the time was right. However, it didn't happen overnight. It took over a year for us to conceive. Waiting was hard. When I decided I wanted a child or two, I wanted them *right now*! If you've waited for anything, you know the impatience, the anxiety, the depression that an extended wait can bring. How the wait can begin to be a weight.

I don't want to volunteer at the school, because my husband is candidating for a new job, in a different city. I don't want to commit and then not be able to follow through.

I'll wait to paint the house—we may be moving sooner rather than later.

I don't want to apply for the promotion. I may not be living in this city when it's announced.

Why bother trying to make friends? We'll end up leaving anyway.

What if I get a new job and then get pregnant?

The longer the wait, the deeper the doubt goes. Fear starts to take root and then digs deep into your heart and soul. You begin to question everything about this particular desire, hope, or whatever it is you are waiting for.

Waiting is never easy, yet God uses it again and again as a tool of refinement. Waiting can draw our hearts closer to Him. Or it can drive us far from Him. It really hangs on how we interpret the wait and what we do with it.

Looking back I can see the struggle I had with God as we waited for children. There was a continual back and forth movement on my end. God never moved or changed His mind. He stood there and waited for me. I would move toward Him, only to move back, away from Him. My heart would question, doubt, and fear. When I trusted, I would step closer to Him, walk alongside Him.

A decade has passed, and I can see now that I was struggling with two questions, questions that we all ask ourselves as we wait: What are we learning about ourselves as we wait? What are we learning about God?

Sarah, the wife of Abraham, wrestled with this too. She spent many years—decades—waiting. Waiting for a promise to be fulfilled even though it seemed hopeless. A child was promised to an old couple who had never been able to have children. Like many women would, Sarah struggled in her wait.

WAITING AND ATTITUDE

Waiting can bring out the worst in us. It exposes what's in our hearts and minds, things we'd rather keep hidden, in the dark. My heart was petulant. I looked this word up. It's defined by *Collins English Dictionary* as "irritable, impatient, or sullen in a peevish or capricious way."[15] Yeah, that about sums up my attitude and behaviour many times while I wait. It's not a very nice description. Children are often petulant because they don't know any better. I'm an adult, yet I act like a child as I wait.

It wasn't just in the waiting to have a family either. I've waited for many things over the last four decades. Besides waiting for a child, I have most often waited in terms of ministry. Waiting for the Lord to direct us or move us. Waiting for release. I have waited for God to lead me in my own ministry. I have been irritable, impatient, sullen, and peevish. I don't think I've ever gone into a wait with an attitude of "Hey! A wait! Wow, let's see what God's gonna do!" It's a little unrealistic to be that positive. But I could improve my attitude. Peevish is not nice to be around. Sullen just makes people want to run from you—or slap you!

Although Sarah is described in the Bible as having great faith, she also had her bad days. For years she watched as family and friends had babies. Their families grew and grew. Sarah waited and waited. Nothing.

John MacArthur in his book *Twelve Extraordinary Women* writes, "She could be impatient, temperamental, conniving, cantankerous, cruel, flighty, pouty, jealous, erratic, unreasonable, a whiner, a complainer or a nag. By no means was she always the perfect model of godly grace and meekness."[16] *Petulant.* I'm so glad we get an honest look at Sarah's struggles. I can connect with this woman because she was just like me. She wasn't a super saint who was meek and good *all the time*! The Bible lets us see her authentically as she lived out her journey here on earth. That doesn't excuse bad behaviour, but it tells me that God understands me. He's seen it all before, and there's nothing that He can't handle. Even my petulance!

Waiting can also bring about major doubt, which can put a crimp in our relationship with God and others. I know I've had times of doubting in my waits. As we struggled with fertility I doubted whether I could be a good mother. I doubted God and His goodness. Why would He put this desire in my heart *when it wasn't there before* and then not let it be fulfilled? When we waited in some tough ministry circumstances, I doubted that God had our best interests at heart. Why make us go through this? It hurt so much, I wasn't sure we could recover from the wounds.

I struggled with people who told us that it was in God's will, people who prayed for God's will to be done—not my own! I felt like saying, "I'm your friend! Why are you praying that way?" Looking back, I know they were right and I was wrong. I couldn't see past my wait, my doubt.

Sarah got caught up in her doubt too. She decided to take things into her own hands. God had made a covenant with her husband that he would be the father of a great nation. Sarah was beyond child-bearing age. She was barren. So she decided to give her maidservant Haggar to Abraham. Perhaps Haggar could conceive the covenant child.

Sarah doubted God and took matters into her own hands. Trying to take control of God's promise, Sarah ruined her relationship with Haggar. We don't know what kind of relationship it was other than mistress and servant. But if there had been any good there, it was gone after Haggar slept with Abraham and conceived his child. Haggar scorned Sarah from then on. In those ancient days, it was a matter of humiliation and shame to not bear children. Haggar rubbed it in Sarah's face. Neither woman could tolerate each other.

Haggar gave birth to a son. Even though Haggar had Abraham's son, Sarah would always be the mistress and Haggar, the servant. It must have been pretty awkward for Abraham too. He had a son whom he loved. He had two women fighting over him, even though Sarah had given Haggar to him. I'm sure family dinners were not pleasant!

IDOL WORSHIP

John MacArthur writes about Sarah, "Every recorded episode of ill temper or strife in her household was related to her frustration about her own barrenness. It ate at her."[17]

I love that description. *It ate at her.* As the wait time was extended, the frustration, doubt, and hopelessness of the whole situation began to eat away at her. In Genesis 12, the Lord told Abraham two things. The first was to leave his home country and go to the land that God would show him. The second was this: "I will make you into a great nation, and I will bless you; I will make your name great, and you will be a blessing. I will bless those who bless you, and whoever curses you I will curse; and all peoples on earth will be blessed through you" (Genesis 12:2–3).

God told Abraham that he would have a son that the covenant blessing would be built on. Several years later—no son for the covenant blessing to be built on. This promise and the wait that ensued gnawed at Sarah.

Do our waits consume us? My struggle with infertility consumed much of me. Other times, it was waiting to hear about a job. It was all I thought about and focused on. Every decision was weighed with that wait in mind. Do you do that too?

This isn't what God wants for us. He wants us to focus on Him. When our waits consume our hearts, our minds, and all of our strength, there's something wrong. It's time for a re-evaluation of our hearts, our priorities.

When we are consumed with that thing we are waiting for, it's become an idol. As daughters of Christ and as ministry leaders, there's no place for idols in our hearts. God is pretty clear on that. I love The Message's interpretation of the first commandment in Exodus 20. It says, "No other gods, only me. No carved gods of any size, shape, or form of anything whatever, whether of things that fly or walk or swim. Don't bow down to them and don't serve them because I am God, your God, and I'm a most jealous God"

God wants all of us focused on Him, not on what we are waiting for, whether it's a child, a ministry opportunity, or an escape.

(Exodus 20:3–5 MSG). He wants to be what consumes us. God wants all of us focused on Him, not on what we are waiting for, whether it's a child, a ministry opportunity, or an escape. These are all good, but not if they take God off the throne of our lives. Not if they steal our hearts.

In Luke 10:27 the doctor gives us the prescription for idol worship or being consumed with what we want, hope for, or desire. He tells us to love God with all our heart, soul, strength, and mind. We are to focus on this only. We are never told to give that focus to anything else.

Sometimes we try to play God, like Sarah did, and manipulate circumstances and people to get what we want. It never works. The consequences can be staggering. We've talked about what happened with Haggar and Sarah. It didn't stop with them. It bled down to their children.

If we take God off the throne and sit down instead, it won't be pretty. It's still idol worship, because God is no longer in charge. We think we are. We think we know best. We don't trust God for His timing and His provision. God will use waiting as a way of drawing these idols out of the dark.

Our attitudes in our waiting test the mettle of our hearts. What do we find there as we wait? Peevishness? Irritability? Doubt? Faith?

In my own experience, as I said, it's a back-and-forth movement. I go through times of frustration, petulance, doubt. Then my faith strengthens. My faith is at its strongest when I'm communicating with God.

WHAT DO WE LEARN ABOUT GOD AS WE WAIT?

Sometimes I wonder what God thinks about us. As any parent can you tell, you *love* your kids, but sometimes you wonder why they do what they do. Sometimes you just don't love what they do. There are days when I feel like I'm beating my head against a brick wall. Why do I try? Why bother? They're just going to go and do what they want to anyhow, no matter how many times I tell them or show them differently. It's enough to drive this mama off the deep end! So I wonder what God thinks about us.

My kids love one of the shows on the Disney channel. It's called *Jesse* and it's about a nanny looking after some kids. One day the youngest girl was called out by Jesse for being a diva. The girl looked at Jesse and said, "I just want what I want when I want it!" Isn't that the way it is with us? With Sarah? *We just want what we want when we want it!* But God has different plans than we do, than Sarah and Abraham did. His plans are way beyond a man and his wife who was barren. They go beyond our own lives, the lives of a pastor and his family. They are God-sized. Even in the vastness, He makes plans for us and takes the time to deal very personally with us too, because the thing that matters most is what He created us for, our relationship with Him. Being a pastor's wife, a mom, a ministry leader, an aunt—all these are good, but if there's no relationship with God, then we're left empty. None of those thing will fill the void in our hearts or our souls.

God will use a wait as a tool of refinement, to draw us back to Him. I hope what we learn about God as we wait will make us want to run as fast as we possibly can to the Father who is waiting for us!

GOD NEVER WASTES A WAIT

God does not just idly make us wait. I believe that there is always a purpose for a wait, because I have lived it.

As I mentioned earlier, our first ministry job became the kind you don't ever want. We were embroiled in turmoil and conflict, and the church eventually imploded. Most of the staff left, for varying reasons. The only ones left were my husband, who was the worship pastor, and a couple of part-time staffers. It was hard to stay when everyone else left. We wanted to leave too, but there was no job to go to. We endured a lot of strife in this time.

We waited a year for God to bring along a new job for my husband. He stayed in his position and served God and his church faithfully. At the time, it was painful. But looking back, I see that a very firm foundation in pastoring a church was forged in that wait. My husband learned a lot that year. He learned that it is vital to have a solid, unified board. He learned to never brush off conflict. He learned to deal with it head on, even if that means having uncomfortable conversations. He learned that the only person he had to please was God. He learned to take the high road, even when the mud being slung at him was full of rocks and twigs. Looking back almost two decades later, I see that the wait was no waste. I see a pastor who has been refined by fire and who has an unswerving faith in his calling and his God.

What about your waits? Has God put you and your husband or church in a waiting pattern? What are you learning as you wait? Do you see that what you are learning or have learned has benefited you as you move on to what God has for you next? Take a moment to examine your times of waiting. Look to see what God has done and what wasn't wasted.

GOD'S TIMING IS PERFECT;
HE'S THE GOD OF IMPOSSIBILITIES

In Jeremiah 29:11 we are told that God has a plan and a purpose for our lives. They're for our good. That's the one everyone quotes. But the next two verses are awesome! They say that when we come and pray to Him and seek Him, we'll find Him. God does have a plan for our lives, and it's based on kingdom time, not on the world's time. When we trust in that timing, it can lead us back to God. If we're looking for answers to God's plan for our lives, we're going to seek Him out, right? Won't you? Even if it's just to ask Him "Why?" God can handle your "why?" and any other questions you've got. Instead of turning away from Him with your doubts, He wants you to turn to Him with all your questions and frustration. God's will is always to draw us back to Him, back into relationship with Him, back to His love for us.

As we wait for God to move, will we trust His timing, in His good will for our lives? Again MacArthur brings up a great point. He writes,

> It was natural for her to think God was deliberately withholding children from her. As a matter of fact, He was. When *His* time came for the promise to be fulfilled, no one would be able to deny that this was indeed God's doing. His plan all along was for Sarah to have her first child in her old age, after every prospect of a natural fulfillment of the prophecy was exhausted and after every earthly reason for hope was completely dead. Thus YHWH would put His power on display.[18]

God's plan is always for His glory, and sometimes He brings us along for the ride. Waiting can make the result much more spectacular than it would have been had it happened right when we wanted it to. When Sarah had a child at age ninety, there was no doubt that only God could have done it. *The Expositor's Bible Commentary* says that not only was it unlikely that Sarah could conceive, it was impossible.[19]

What truly amazes me is that when Abraham was ninety-nine and Sarah was eighty-nine, God reiterated the promise, the impossible, to Abraham. And this time, He named Sarah—old, barren Sarah—as the mother of the child. God told Abraham, "As for Sarai your wife, you are no longer to call her Sarai; her name will be Sarah. I will bless her and will surely give you a son by her. I will bless her so that she will be the mother of nations; kings of peoples will come from her" (Genesis 17:15–16). Because with God, nothing is impossible.

How many times have the things we're waiting for seemed impossible? Sarah laughed when one of the divine visitors said that in a year she would have a son: "Abraham and Sarah were already very old by this time, and Sarah was past the age of childbearing. So Sarah laughed to herself as she thought, 'After I am worn out and my lord is old, will I now have this pleasure?'" (Genesis 18:11–12). When we are finally told that what we've been waiting for is going to happen, what's our reaction? I think my first instinct is disbelief. "No way. It's not going to happen." It's a form of self-protection because I don't want to be disappointed again. I've been down that road one too many times.

Some people cry with relief. Some people laugh. "Stunned" would be a good description. Our hearts tremble in the face of impossibility. We are vulnerable once again.

What if the answer is no? As I've struggled with waiting there have been times when being okay with the answer no seemed more impossible than what I was waiting for! Sometimes the attitude adjustment is the bigger miracle that needs to happen.

Do we need to step back and get a different perspective of our wait? Maybe the job that is going to best suit both our husband and us isn't available yet. There's a few more things that need to happen. Maybe we need to stay put because we're closer to family and a support system that we're going to need in the future. God knows why we wait, and His timing is perfect for our lives. He has a will, and *impossible* isn't even an issue for Him!

GOD ALWAYS KEEPS HIS PROMISES

I am sure that by now Sarah thought God was going to fulfill His promise some other way. I don't think she doubted that God would do what He promised, but she just couldn't wrap her mind around *how* He would do it.

We've all struggled with this, haven't we? You know God is faithful to His Word, but you just can't figure out how it's going to come about. You still have a tiny mustard seed of faith that believes. Against all odds, you believe that God will do as He promised. I think Sarah deep down had that tiny mustard seed of faith. God had made a covenant with Abraham. There was no denying it. She believed that God was faithful to that promise. "She sometimes vacillated, but she ultimately persevered against unbelievable obstacles, and the steadfastness of her faith became the central feature of her legacy."[20]

Our youngest son asked me one night why God didn't answer his prayer. I had to stop for a minute because the same question had been on my mind! Honestly, I didn't want to discourage him. My own faith was lacking at the moment. I said a quick "Help" prayer.

And the Holy Spirit gave me some divine wisdom.

"Honey," I said, "you know how sometimes you ask Mommy and Daddy for something? And because we want to do what's best for you, sometimes the answer is yes, no, or wait. It's the same with God. Sometimes He says yes, sometimes no, and other times, wait."

Whatever the answer, God has promised that He will never leave us or forsake us. He doesn't leave us alone in the waiting room of life.

Looking back over almost two decades, I see that God has kept this promise to me. He has walked beside us as we went through church splits, conflict, loss, betrayal. He has walked beside us as we rejoiced with fellow believers as they discovered who they were in Christ, as prayers were answered, and as they waited. Sometimes we just have to take a minute and *remember!* Throughout Scripture, God continually calls us to remember what He has done. He tells the Israelites to write it on their foreheads and doorposts (Deuteronomy 6:6–9, 11:18–20). To tell their children. Remembering His faithfulness, His love, keeps us from stumbling while we wait. It builds our hearts strong. We see God's glory and His power and His majesty when we remember. We start to look for it while we wait because we remember it!

God didn't leave Sarah and Abraham alone through those thirty-three years of waiting. He hasn't left me or you alone either. He's sitting right beside us. Lying in our sickbed with us. Waiting, holding our hands as we hurt, as we wait.

Hebrews 11 records it in verse 11: "And by faith even Sarah, who was past childbearing age, was enabled to bear children because she considered him faithful who had made the promise." I want my legacy to be one of faith in a God of impossibilities, who always keeps His promises and who can handle my doubt, my questions. I want to instill this in my children.

"Now to him who is able to do immeasurably more than all we ask or imagine, according to his power that is at work within us, to him be glory in all the church and in Christ Jesus throughout all generations, for ever and ever!" (Ephesians 3:20–21).

WAITING FOR A HOME

The other thing that Sarah had to wait for was a home. She had one, and then she didn't. God's calling on her husband took her away from her home and her family. God was leading Abraham to a new place. To a new covenant. Sarah was required to follow.

If you are a pastor's wife, you've probably been in this position. Waiting for something new: A new home. A new city. A new church. You have a home, and then you don't. It requires leaving family and friends. You are going on to something new.

"The Lord had said to Abram, 'Go from your country, your people and your father's household and to the land I will show you'" (Genesis 12:1). Our husbands' calling can sound a lot like this. It's not so much what is said but who says it. Isn't this why we follow our husbands? Why we believe in their calling, believe in God? Isn't it why Sarah picked up her household and followed Abraham to a big question mark? They didn't even have a destination. Sarah fully believed in and trusted God and her husband.

If I didn't have faith in God and in my husband and his call to ministry, I don't think I would have followed him across the country like I have. It's what keeps me going at times. I trust that God is leading our family. If I had any doubts about my husband's calling or his character, I would quit.

In fact, I have at times encouraged him to quit—or at least evaluate again his call to ministry. Every time, he has come back to me sure of his call. Sure of his God. I can follow that.

I think Sarah was the same. John MacArthur writes, "Life on the road was not something Sarah was accustomed to; it was something she had to learn to embrace."[21] I can totally relate. Moving around takes a lot of effort, both physical and mental. It is exhausting. My family never moved when I was a kid. My parents lived within a ten-mile radius of where they grew up. So I wasn't really accustomed to moving either. It's something I've had to learn to do. I embrace certain parts of it and grieve the rest. But it's the belief that we are part of something bigger, of a faithful God who has called us to do this job, that keeps us going.

We've had five major moves in twenty years. We've crossed provinces. We've lived in major metropolises and smaller cities. We've met some very interesting people. We've made friends, some for a season and some for life. For the most part, I haven't minded moving. It always presented itself as a fresh start. I usually hated my job by the time moving day arrived, so I was relieved to be able to leave. That was a plus.

The same can be said for houses and apartments. Moving always provides a chance to get something new and better suited to us. It's also an opportunity to purge the junk and extras we don't use. I always enjoy this process.

There are many other pluses to moving around, but there are some major minuses too. Leaving family and friends is difficult, especially if you have a support system in place. Leaving that support is hard for everyone, and if you don't have a similar structure in the new place, your world can be turned upside down for some time.

It's hard not having friends to talk to and lean on when you move. I've found it takes several years to make friends who will make a difference in my life. This may be totally different for you, but that has been my experience.

If you're a pastor's wife, each new church provides challenges: meeting new people and telling your story again and again. Trying to remember names and who is related to whom. As an introvert, I've been overwhelmed at times and generally just wanted to hide out in my husband's office. Occasionally I have!

It may mean getting used to a new style of worship or a change in service. Office hours and what's expected of your husband can totally change your world. There are so many "new" things that it can feel overwhelming. Susan Miller writes that after hearing a pastor's wife tell her story, "That was the first time I realized the kind of struggle so many pastors' wives have in moving, and yet people in their congregation just expect them to jump in and start serving them. We need to be sensitive to their needs; they have to adjust just like anyone else."[22] Fortunately I have been blessed to be in some churches that gave me time to find my own niche. It's one of the biggest blessings a church has ever bestowed on me. I'm very grateful that at the majority of places I wasn't pushed into a role I didn't fit. It really wouldn't have ended well for any of us. Maybe they saw that in me!

But if you're expected to "jump in and start serving," that's tough, because moving involves grieving what you've lost in the move. It's much like a death, depending on how deeply rooted you were. We wouldn't expect a new widow to just jump in and get her hands dirty serving, would we? I don't think so.

Our last move proved to be the hardest. I really don't think there is a good age to move kids, unless they are babies. Our boys were seven and nine at the time. Like any human, they mourned for their friends, their school, their home. There was depression, anxiety, and anger. All the stages of grieving came and went multiple times. After two years, the tears and pleas to move back diminished. Memories became happy, not sad. They made new friends and new memories and started to thrive, not merely survive. But it took time.

I wasn't prepared for that. I wasn't prepared for my own reaction and grief. I mourned for the boys, but I also mourned for myself. I missed my own friends. I missed being able to hang out with friends after a last-minute phone call. We don't have that in our new place. It may come with time. I hope so. I also left my twin sister, and that was hard. It had been wonderful being close to her for the previous eight years. The world seemed right and good when I was near her.

I'm sure that Sarah had many of the emotions we feel when we move and when we wait for the next ministry job or opportunity. She followed her husband faithfully and waited, trusting in God's faithfulness. Can the same be said of me? Of us?

I know God can handle my anger, my frustration, and my loneliness. I've had my "discussions" with Him. I've ranted, I've cried, and I've pleaded. But in the end, I know beyond a shadow of a doubt that we have followed His call. That wherever He leads us, He will be faithful. So I follow Mark because I trust him and, even more than that, I trust the God we both serve.

Chapter Five

Grateful

Every once in a while, I stumble across something on social media that convinces me that there is some good in the Internet. A few years back, I found a friend of a friend's thankfulness photo diary. They are more common today, but at the time I had never seen one before. I was intrigued. As I followed her daily progress, I began to contemplate posting my own daily photo and why I was thankful. But something held me back. Did I really want to commit to something like that?

After about five months of following this page, I was on the verge of making my own thankfulness album. And then, out of the blue, the day after I decided I was going to do it, I got an email from a friend on the west coast. She wrote, "I've been reading this book, and I keep thinking that you would really enjoy it. Have you heard of it or read it yet?" The book was *One Thousand Gifts,* by Ann Voskamp. It's a book about living a life of gratitude. I bought the book and started to read it.

In my mind, this was no coincidence. I felt that God was calling me to a life of gratitude and thankfulness. Once again we weren't in the best ministry spot, and we were tired and weary. I needed to change my attitude and perspective. Voskamp's story and life resonated with me. We had many similar experiences, from the death of a sibling to anxiety attacks starting at a young age. I saw healing and wholeness in her story, and I wanted what she had. It felt like it could be the next step in my journey to healing.

So I started a Facebook album called *A Year of Thankfulness*. Each day I posted a picture and a statement of what I was thankful for. As well, I devoured Voskamp's book and started a journal to count to 1,000 gifts.

I did the project to get myself in a better place, and I wasn't prepared for the response to my daily posts. People thanked me for doing it and were inspired themselves to intentionally live a little more gratefully. This was supposed to help me, not anyone else. But if God is in it, He always leaks out. You can't hold Him in. Scripture says that if we don't give praise to God, the rocks and the streams will cry out.

In the book of Luke, there's the story of a woman who exuded the love of God because she was loved and forgiven. She had a heart full of gratitude and love.

> *A woman in that town who lived a sinful life learned that Jesus was eating at the Pharisee's house, so she came there with an alabaster jar of perfume. As she stood behind him at his feet weeping, she began to wet his feet with her tears. Then she wiped them with her hair, kissed them and poured perfume on them.* (Luke 7:37–38)

This woman had led a sinful life. Most commentaries agree that she was likely a prostitute. At some point she had turned from her sinful life. She believed that what Jesus said was true—she had been forgiven.[23] She was so grateful that she had to express it somehow. Matthew Henry points out that "she came to acknowledge her obligations to him."[24] In other words, she wanted to thank Him and to show her love for Him. "This was what our Lord Jesus took special notice of, that she *loved much*."[25]

Jesus noted the obvious difference between the woman and his host, Simon the Pharisee:

> *"Do you see this woman? I came into your house. You did not give me any water for my feet, but she wet my feet with her tears and*

wiped them with her hair. You did not give me a kiss, but this woman, from the time I entered, has not stopped kissing my feet. You did not put oil on my head, but she has poured perfume on my feet. Therefore, I tell you, her many sins have been forgiven—as her great love has shown. But whoever has been forgiven little loves little." (Luke 7:44–47)

This woman couldn't contain herself. As Alice Mathews says in her book *A Woman God Can Lead,* "Once again Simon had ignored his duty as host by not anointing his guest with oil. Once again a grateful, forgiven woman did what the calculating Pharisee chose not to do."[26] She loved Jesus by anointing Him with not only perfume but her tears as well. I think her tears were an outward expression of her heart, a heart full of gratitude and love. It was a way of giving her heart back to Jesus. She came humbly.[27] Love, thankfulness, and humility are a powerful combination.

HUMILITY

For two consecutive years I posted daily what I was thankful for, and I learned a thing or two. The first thing I realized was that I was definitely slowing down and noticing things. For example, I had never really thought much about the wildlife around me. I thought that taking time to notice squirrels playing in the trees was—well, what *was* the point? I didn't have time to slow down and put aside my own agenda. I was too important. The stuff I had to do was important, was it not?

As I hunted for things to be thankful for, I started to see—really see—nature. God was using the world He created to draw me in and slow me down, to make me see how big He is and how small I am and that it's not all about me. But at the same time, these gifts were for me to enjoy—if I'd only stop and put aside my own importance and schedule.

I started to enjoy the birdsong in the early morning. I loved sitting on the back deck, drinking my morning coffee and enjoying the green, the trees, and the birds and squirrels. I started to stop and watch the sun set. We had some spectacular sunsets in very flat Windsor, Ontario. I counted five rainbows that summer.

These gifts didn't just add up to another number in my journal or pictures to post. They started to talk to me about the God who created them.

These gifts didn't just add up to another number in my journal or pictures to post. They started to talk to me about the God who created them. They told me that He wants to speak with me, and some days He does this through the world around me. His creation told me that He is a master artist. His works are incredible and never identical. He is a God of uniqueness, colour, and beauty.

These things spoke to my soul. I had needed to stop. And look. And listen. Stopping takes humility because many times it means laying aside what you want to do. I would not have seen the beauty if I hadn't learned humility.

The sinful woman had learned humility. She was in the presence of her Saviour. He had rescued her from a life of sin and yet loved her still. She didn't come in brashly to Jesus; instead she entered quietly, meekly. She stood behind Him and started to weep. She didn't address Him or call attention to herself. Matthew Henry says that she did not look Jesus in the face but came behind Him and performed the task of a "maidservant."[28] She did so lovingly. Gratefully.

THANKFULNESS AND SACRIFICE

The other thing I learned is that being thankful takes training. We have to train ourselves to look for His gifts. Some days this is not easy. Other days overflow. But we have to practice and train our minds and thoughts. Some days it's a sacrifice, a sacrifice of praise. It costs us something to lift up our eyes and hands and faces and say thank you.

The woman who came to Jesus knew the cost of saying thank you. Her infamy preceded her; Simon, whose house she entered to anoint Jesus, said, "If this man were a prophet, he would know who is touching him and what kind of woman she is—that she is a sinner" (Luke 7:39). You can hear the scorn and derision in the voice of Simon the Pharisee. Oh, he knew what she was, and so did everyone else in that room. Trash.

In order to see Jesus, this woman risked public scorn. She knew that people wouldn't be so forgiving, and it cost her to enter this Pharisee's house to anoint Jesus. I'm sure she was aware of the stares, the not-so-whispered comments, the elbow nudges. She did so anyway because she wanted to thank Jesus. She wanted to show how much she loved Him. Nothing else mattered. Not the stares, the comments, or the disapproval. Only Jesus.

Hebrews says, "Through Jesus, therefore, let us continually offer to God a sacrifice of praise—the fruit of lips that openly profess his name" (Hebrews 13:15). I like the New American Standard Bible version of this verse: "Through Him then, let us continually offer up a sacrifice of praise to God, that is, the fruit of lips that give thanks to His name." Praise, being thankful, can cost us something at times. Not in the "I got something; now I must give something back" way. Paul said, "Sing and make music from your heart to the Lord, always giving thanks to God the Father for everything, in the name of our Lord Jesus Christ" (Ephesians 5:19–20). If we actually follow that concept, it's going to cost.

In those two years when I posted about thankfulness, there were days when I didn't feel too thankful. I didn't want to sing and make music in my heart to the Lord. The boys had been fighting, or money was tight. Sickness happened. People betrayed us. I wasn't in the mood for thankfulness. Those days I had to dig deep to find even one thing I was thankful for. In doing so, I had to change my attitude. I had to give up my grumbling. My pride. My "right" to whatever it was that I thought I should have. (It was a good thing that I was learning about humility already!) There was a price.

I think of stories I've heard about families at funeral services who choose to worship God. Even though they are hurting, grieving a loved one, they choose to lift their hands, their eyes, their faces, to God. It's a sacrifice, but they do it willingly, just like that sinful woman. She chose to go to a place where she was not welcome in order to thank her Lord and Saviour with the fruit of her lips. Do my lips offer up this fruit on the hard days? Or even on the days when everything is zipping along smoothly? It's easy to forget to say thank you on those days too.

As pastors' wives, our very lives can be given in sacrifice. As I've said, I had to let go of some of my dreams. The road I've walked is not the one I'd have willingly chosen as we became fishers of men and women and children. Careers, dreams, vacations, and money have had to be sacrificed on the altar of our lives—given over and released. It has cost something of us.

What have you had to let go of and lay down before the cross? Living through these decisions is not easy, and it's definitely hard to be thankful for everything, at all times. I think I'm just starting to understand humility. It has to come first so that I can take that step to lay down my sacrifice and then give thanks for it.

Sometimes we're not the ones who directly make the sacrifices, which makes it even harder to let go. Ministry can involve a lot of change. At one point, my husband and I felt that God was calling our family to a new place and ministry position. Both my husband and I were excited— it was time, time to move on. Our two young boys weren't so thrilled. I wasn't naively thinking that everything would come up smelling like roses—I had moved enough times to know better—but I didn't think that my children would be the ones who had to make the most sacrifices. I didn't expect that at all.

As a result of the transition in ministry, the boys have had questions about God. It scared me. What if they start to blame God? What if they can't get past this struggle and they leave church when they get older? I've heard the stories from other pastors' wives. There's no guarantee here.

I have grieved with my boys as they mourned the lives they left behind. Sacrifice. I *believe* this is where God called us. I don't pretend to understand why the boys have struggled so much. But I choose to believe that God has brought us here and will not forsake us. Like Stormie Omartian writes in her book *The Power of a Praying Parent*, "Lord...I know that *You* brought us here and You will not leave my children forsaken."[29] I cling to Psalm 9:10: "Those who know your name trust in you, for you, LORD, have never forsaken those who seek you." Being thankful doesn't equal easy, but what it does do is make your heart tender toward what God is doing in your life.

But what happens if we choose a different path? In Luke, I think it's clear. We can become like the Pharisee. Simon was too busy judging the woman and Jesus. His soul was wrapped up in appearances instead of searching out the truth of the heart of the one who sat right in his house! He was blind. As Mathews says, Simon chose not to honour Jesus as his guest. At that time, it was customary for the host to offer water for foot washing, to welcome his guest with a kiss, and to anoint his head with oil. Simon did none of these for Jesus. Instead, the woman did it. She chose to do it out of thankfulness.[30]

I have to ask myself, am I a Pharisee at heart? Do I sit and judge others and Jesus? I admit to being ticked off at times that Jesus offers forgiveness to all people rather than being thankful for His grace. Because deep down, there are some people I struggle with. A lot of them are Christians. In my arrogance, I forget that I'm no different than the next girl. I'm in need of His grace. I need His cleansing blood to clean up this wreck. Why am I judging how He chooses to extend His grace to another? I have become a Pharisee, without humility, thankfulness, or love. I think I know all about those I'm thumbing my nose at—their lives, their struggles—when in fact I haven't got a clue.

We have a neighbour who has dogs that bark. A lot. One day, my kids accidentally kicked a ball over the fence into her yard. She picked it up and said over the fence, "Is this yours?" The boys answered yes. She threw it back to them—damaged. The dogs had punctured the ball.

The following winter the boys were out in the backyard with friends. I guess some snowballs went over the fence, because the dogs were barking. She came to our door that night. She was understanding but asked that we see her point of view. The dogs had come from the Humane Society and had been traumatized by a previous owner. She was trying to restore them. Upon reflecting on the ball incident, I think she thought the boys had thrown the ball at the dog. They hadn't, but she didn't know that. She's pregnant with her first child. She's going to find out that balls go over fences accidentally. I could give her a little of the grace that has been extended to me instead of judging because I think I have all the answers. In my mind I'd already tried and convicted her of just being mean and cruel. I have the heart of a Pharisee.

LOVE

Jesus had been accused of being a friend of tax collectors and sinners (Luke 7:34). Simon alludes to this as he thinks to himself that if Jesus were really a prophet He would know who this woman was (Luke 7:39). There's no love in Simon's heart. Not for Jesus, whom he is doubting, and not for the woman, whom he is judging. Simon is only concerned with appearances, but not really his own. He has snubbed Jesus by not being a good host, yet he is unconcerned about this. I think he really thinks he is above them all.

But Jesus is the story here. A friend to sinners, tax collectors, and all the other fringe people. He tells the woman that her sins are forgiven and her faith has saved her. To go in peace (Luke 7:48, 50). She already knows that her sins are forgiven. I think Jesus says it so that everyone else there, including Simon, will know it. Jesus assures the woman of her salvation, commends her faith, and then blesses her. "Go in peace." It's beautiful. It's filled with love for her. I can only imagine how she feels. Euphoric, I'm sure, but humbled too. Loved. Blessed.

I hope that as a ministry couple we get accused of extending too much grace, love, and kindness like Jesus did. I hope I'm not a friend only to other Christians and stay away from sinners. As fishers of men and women, we are to go out into the world, and that means out beyond the Christian world. I hope I never get to be like Simon and the other Pharisees who stayed in their own little group and world so they did not become "unclean." I love the fact that Jesus was indeed a friend to the messed up, the sinners, and the fringe people. He moved freely and gracefully about those circles. That He didn't just rub shoulders with the religious elite. Instead He hung out with fishermen, tax collectors, and women with sketchy pasts. They were His inner circle, not the religious officials. Those were the people who shunned him, the ones who thought they were "in the know." Turns out they didn't know a thing.

How does the call to become missional have anything to do with a grateful heart? As God called me to be thankful, I started to learn humility, as I've said. A thankful heart is not proud. As pride took a hike and I saw God in His creation and how He uses it to communicate with us, I became thankful and filled with love for Him. Out of that love came the ability to love others. As my friend put it, He gave me new eyes for His creation and then new eyes for His people. I firmly believe that I wouldn't have the one without the other.

As an introvert and a glass-half-empty kind of girl, I haven't always had a heart for people. In truth, a lot of times people just bug me. They make me uncomfortable; they mess stuff up. I'm arrogant and unloving. God is using the road to thankfulness to soften my heart. First He had to break it, as I've talked about, but then He had to make it thankful. "Pride goes before destruction, a haughty spirit before a fall" (Proverbs 16:18). But humility and gratitude lead to love, love for God, and the knowledge of His love for me. Out of that love comes love for others.

This is what God has called us to. James calls it the royal law. "Love your neighbor as yourself" (James 2:8). "Royal" means it comes from the King. It's a decree. It's not to be taken lightly or discarded. We are commanded to love our neighbour as ourselves. As Jay Pathak and Dave Runyon say in their book *The Art of Neighboring, neighbour* actually means the people who live next door to us.[31] "When Jesus was asked to reduce everything important into one command, he gave us a simple and powerful plan that, if acted on, would literally change the world… By becoming good neighbors, we become who we're supposed to be."[32] It's not easy to step out and get uncomfortable with strangers, but when we do, love goes into action. We become better neighbours, and our neighbourhoods get safer, kinder, and more neighbourly. It's a win-win for everyone. By showing love and kindness to others we become God's hands and feet. We get to know God better.

For instance, I once bought some fresh flowers for myself. Three small bouquets were on sale, and God gave me a nudge to give one of them to the neighbour across the street, a recent widow. The thankfulness experiment had brought me more in tune with God, and I felt that nudge. So I took the bouquet to my neighbour. I thought about letting my son do it when he got home from school, but I knew if I left it too long, I'd chicken out. So I delivered it.

On the way back I was trying to figure out if there was maybe something important happening in her life that I didn't know about it. Then it hit me. Father's Day was that coming weekend, the first without her husband, the father of her children. I hadn't realize the significance of the date, but God had! He wanted her to know that He loved her and hadn't forgotten her. It showed me how much God cares for us and that He is still taking care of the orphans and widows. They are still important to Him. He gave me the privilege of catching a glimpse of that.

The royal law is important. We make excuses to ignore it. We make it optional. We need to get our hands dirty a bit more. Get in the mess of other people's lives, some of whom we may be a little afraid of. We need to be generous. As ministry wives, we have the opportunity and influence to lead the way out the front doors of our churches and into our communities, our cities. We can bring the sweet fragrance of Jesus to our neighbours through relationships with them, not so much by our words but by our actions.

Like the woman who had sinned, we need to venture into places that are a bit awkward for us. My neighbour with the dogs? I give her kudos for even coming to our door to discuss what happened in a friendly manner. I'm not sure I'd have done it. I probably would have huddled in and complained to everyone but her. She took a risk. We are all better for it.

So maybe it's time to venture in where we don't necessarily fit. People are not flocking into the church. Too many think that the church is made up of Simons. Instead, God's church should reflect the sinful woman. We, the people who make up the church, should be weeping because we are forgiven. Because we are saved. We are free of our bondage to sin. Grateful hearts and actions should reflect that gratitude. We should be whispering "Jesus, Jesus, Jesus." Our lives should be like a fragrant perfume that permeates the world around us. That's what the church—God's bride—should look like!

The grace and love that Jesus showered on this woman—that's the greatest perfume of all. What would happen if the church showed grace and love to sinners like Jesus did instead of judging them like Simon did? Jesus said that we are to feed the hungry, give drink to the thirsty, clothe those who are naked, and visit the sick and incarcerated. And when we do these things? "The King will reply, 'Truly I tell you, whatever you did for one of the least of these brothers and sisters of mine, you did for me'" (Matthew 25:40). In doing so, we are fulfilling the first law, to love God with all our heart, mind, and soul.

Loving others equals loving God, even those who are unlovable, have noisy dogs, or are labelled in some way by the world and by Christians. Sinners. If *all* churches in North America actually followed this law—I'm not saying that none do; there are some who live this out beautifully—how different would our world look? Our communities? Our neighbourhoods? As pastors' wives, we can be positive influences living out of grateful hearts that weep because of the grace and forgiveness we have experienced, rather than out of cold, judging, pharisaical hearts.

Chapter Six

Courageous

"You are where you are for such a time as this
—not to gain anything—
but to risk everything."
—Ann Voskamp

I've always been a scaredy cat. Fear is one of my earliest memories: I had a nightmare that my twin sister was lost in a house fire. I was probably only about three or four at the time. The memories of that nightmare haunted me for days afterwards. Then later, afraid of the dark, I'd hide under my covers, getting hot and sweaty, only coming up for air when I couldn't breathe. I don't do scary movies. I'm afraid to fly, although I will when there's no other choice. I don't like crowded places or too many people. I'm afraid of elevators and high places. I'm afraid of deep water. The list could go on and on, I'm embarrassed to say!

The anxiety attacks started when I was ten. I always had to be near a door or at the end of an aisle so I could get out quickly if I needed to. Growing up, I thought I was weird. I tried to hide it from people, even though at times I'd act irrational. I'd get angry and hysterical for no apparent reason. I remember being at a concert and freaking out because our seats were too high up. It was crowded, and I couldn't calm down. I refused to sit there, so I spent most of the concert at the back of the behind after the exile may have assimilated into Persian culture over time, or they may have just stayed under the radar. Not making much noise, quietly going about their business and religion. We don't know for sure. No one knew her true identity. What would have happened if someone had found out and told the king? We never find that out, but it must have been a nagging worry in the back of Esther's mind. It would have made me extremely cautious about who I trusted.

Esther had a lot to contend with, but she didn't cower in fear. She had a heart of courage rather than one of anxiety. Maybe that's why Esther is the only female besides Ruth with a book in the Bible named after her.

SAFETY

I could stand to learn a few lessons from Esther. This is just a snippet of her story too! Safe—how we value this state of being. Safety is good, but at times I think I make it my idol. God did not call us to be safe. He doesn't put a premium on our safety or what we think might make us safe. Maybe that's why He needs people who are willing to risk it all for Him. Willing to get out of their safety nets and comfort zones and go out into an extremely unsafe world. To go on a mission trip. To be the voice of truth in the workplace. To become a missionary. A pastor. A pastor's wife!

God had plans for Esther, and they put her in the direct line of danger. God doesn't shy away from danger. He doesn't want us to either. He is our rock and strength, a very present help in times of trouble. He wants us to rely on Him, not ourselves. He wants us to have faith and to trust Him. To grow. As parents, we want our children to grow. To trust us. There is so much fear-mongering in this world, especially when it comes to child-rearing! They have to be strapped in, wrapped in armour, and slathered in SPF 100 sunscreen to do anything these days!

If we're not careful, we'll suffocate our children. They won't learn the essential skills they need to live and thrive in this world if we don't give them some room to breathe. To try new things—sometimes dangerous things. To become independent. To become the warriors God created them to be.

When my guys were little I would see parents at the park who would not let their little ones climb a small ladder unattended. I'm not talking about one- and two-year-olds either. Four- and five-year-olds were told no, they could not climb that ladder by themselves. My eldest boy is a climber. I read somewhere that I should let him climb. Let him be a boy. Let him test his ability. So I did. While other parents were gasping, I let him climb the big ladders. He was sure-footed and unafraid. He didn't even blink at the risks he took. To him, they weren't risks to be avoided. Instead he saw adventures, opportunities, challenges to conquer. As an adult, I've lost this sense of adventure that my son exhibits. I avoid risks. My desire for adventure as a young adult has evaporated as I cling to safety. I think God wants us to let go of safety so we will try and do anything, like I did with my son climbing at the playground.

Esther's story is one of adventure and opportunity to go and do and conquer. It could have been just the opposite. It could have been about fear, self-pity, and self-absorption. It's interesting that Esther's story begins with the telling of another woman's story. Vashti, queen of Persia, refused to go to her husband when he called for her. This event set in motion the circumstances that led to Esther becoming the new queen of Persia. Esther, right from the outset, was in hot water precisely because she was *not* Vashti.

COMPARISON

It's the palimpsest effect. Never heard of it? It's not that common, but the word has such a great meaning, and it describes Esther's story so well. *Collin's English Dictionary* defines *palimpsest* as "a manuscript on which two or more successive texts have been written, each one being erased to make room for the next."[34]

Timothy Beal, in his book *Book of Hiding: Gender, Ethnicity, Annihilation and Esther*, writes, "As the reader moves out of chapter 1 and into the 'main story' or 'narrative proper,' the beginning '*leaves the mark of erasure.*'"[35] Beale is speaking about the exit of Vashti. He says,

Derrida's [whose theories Beale is reflecting on] reflections help articulate another dimension of the problematics of identity politics in the story; the other can never "fit" cozily with the same, for it is neither the same nor the opposite; the logic of the same will work either to reduce it (to sameness or opposition) or to erase it, but neither can be entirely successful. There will always be a trace, a remainder, an erasure mark, the sign of a departure of something that is not part of the present order of things.[36]

He goes on to write, "Think of the book of Esther as a kind of palimpsest: a story is written, then erased, and then a new story is written over the old, erased one."[37] A story is written in Esther, chapter 1, about Vashti and the king and her refusal to go to him. Vashti is banished, so her story is erased, and Esther's story is written over it.

This doesn't sound dangerous or even risky. But if you've ever had to live your life overtop of someone else's, you know how paralyzing it can be. It feels risky being yourself. There are so many things to be afraid of—fear you won't make the grade, won't be good enough. As a pastor's wife, comparing yourself to other women in the church or a former pastor's wife can be debilitating. Some people will compare you, and others won't. You can't please everyone.

If *I'm* the one comparing myself and listening to others, then I'm setting myself up for trouble. God created each of us unique, no two alike, so when He calls us out to do something, He's not asking us to be a copy of someone else. Maybe you've been called to teach Bible studies. That doesn't mean you have to be a Beth Moore or a Kay Arthur. You may have a skill set that is completely different from theirs, and God wants you to use it to teach Bible studies. I believe that it's the women and men who are not afraid to be different, to use what

God created each of us unique, no two alike, so when He calls us out to do something, He's not asking us to be a copy of someone else.

they're gifted with, who make the most difference in the lives of others and in the world. They step out in faith and do what God wants them to do, no matter how different it may seem or look to others. Just look through the books of the Bible! Joseph interpreted dreams. Daniel was faithful to his God through his eating and prayer life. He and his friends refused to bow down to idols. All the prophets were laughed at, and worse. Esther is another example, a woman who was different but was used mightily by God.

Vashti was "lovely to look at" (Esther 1:11), which is why she was summoned by the king. He wanted to show her off. The Bible says that Esther "had a lovely figure and was beautiful" (Esther 2:7). I wonder if she saw herself that way? Had she ever seen the former queen, Vashti, before? If she had, did Esther compare herself to Vashti? I wonder if when she was taken by the royal guards to the palace to be in the contest, she worried about her looks. Sometimes the most physically beautiful women are the most insecure.

Esther was up against all of Persia's most gorgeous virgins. She was competing with a past memory and a present bevy of beauties. Was she beautiful enough to entice the king? This contest wasn't for a fake crown and trophy. The stakes were high. Her life depended on winning. Victory meant becoming queen and having a say in her life. Defeat meant being one of the king's concubines, a glorified prostitute. Her life would have been over.

After Esther became queen, I don't think Vashti just disappeared. Her erasure mark was deep. It's why the contest had been held, to help the king forget Vashti and move on with a new queen. I believe that Esther endured constant comparisons to the former queen by personal attendants, palace workers, court attendants, and the Persian people. She may have had her own Vashti scale that she used for herself. Unfortunately it's in our earthly nature to compare.

I've been dealing with comparison a lot lately. It keeps coming up. Blog after blog and book after book keep talking about how we women too often compare ourselves and compete with one another. It's true! I never thought about myself as a comparer. It's not something I want to admit to, even to myself. For most of my life, I honestly couldn't have cared less whether I wore the latest fashion, had a boyfriend, or an owned a designer whatever. The one area where I consistently compared and judged myself was against the backdrop of career.

Not just any career, either. The one I wanted: writing. Telling a story, having my name right there in black and white. Making a difference in someone's life. Getting paid to do it, and therefore making ends meet. It's hard to be cheerful and well-wishing when someone else gets what you've been waiting for, for what seems like your whole life. I get jealous even of women I don't know. Silly, isn't it? It doesn't make it any less real.

Sometimes I cut them out of my life. I don't read their blogs anymore. If I know them, I avoid, avoid, avoid! Then I don't have to deal with the disappointment of my own life. But that's a lie. If I don't deal with it, it's going to hound me until I do. So I am a comparer.

It makes me feel like a loser. Holding myself up to someone else's standards and high points only makes me feel bad. Most of the time, I don't know their whole story, the struggles, the hurts, and the wounds that are masked in their "success." All I see is what my friend likes to call "their highlight reel." It's only the highlights of their lives that I'm seeing—their successes, accomplishments, and accolades. If I look at my own life, success and applause are very elusive. When they come, they are gone in, well, "fifteen minutes of fame."

Comparing ourselves to others is a dead end. I have concluded that Esther did not spend much time comparing, or else she would not have succeeded in wooing the king, in winning the beauty contest. If I'm too busy comparing, I'm not doing anything else, because I'm paralyzed by all the I-should-haves, I-can'ts, and what-ifs! Esther was different because she was a doer. Her heart was filled with courage, not fear.

ATTITUDE

After Esther was taken to the palace, she could have done nothing. She had the looks. She could have just hoped that her beauty would help her to win. She could have sat in fear and trembling because she was in a tight spot. She did neither of these. Her heart was true and full of courage. It showed in her attitude. Esther 2:8 says that after Esther was taken as part of the harem, she was entrusted to Hegai, the head eunuch. Esther "pleased him and won his favor" (Esther 2:9). In Beth Moore's study on Esther, she points out that the Hebrew wording here is active. Esther gained or took kindness.[38] She was actively gaining favour. There are a few theories about how she went about gaining the favour of Hegai and the other girls in the harem (Esther 2:15). Moore says that it was because of her people skills and manners.[39]

Charles Swindoll in his book *Esther: A Woman of Strength and Dignity* gives a list of traits Esther exhibited that helped her find favour. Among them were an unselfish modesty and authenticity. "She does not succumb to the temptation around her—the superficiality, the selfishness, the seduction, the self-centeredness. She displays an unselfish modesty, an authenticity, amid unparalleled extravagance."[40] I think the young orphaned Hadassah was very much evident here. She didn't lose focus or get distracted by the many luxuries that the palace offered. She was respectful. Esther's character gained her favour with Hegai and those around her.

When it was her turn to go to the king, she asked Hegai what to take with her, and she did only what he advised. She understood that he knew the king best. She was no fool. She tapped into that wisdom. She listened to those above her—not only Hegai but also Mordecai, who came every day to the gate. She was liked because she wasn't moping around.

She obviously stood out from the rest of the pack as someone worthy of being the future queen. Hegai "immediately…provided her with her beauty treatments and special food. He assigned to her seven female attendants selected from the king's palace and moved her and her attendants into the best place in the harem" (Esther 2:9–10). Hegai was gunning for Esther to win, and he equipped her with all the tools to do so. He must have seen something in her to make her worthy of the special attention.

It takes courage to have a good attitude. To be respectful of those in authority over us. It's easy to be in a funk, to fall into self-pity or to sit in fear. It's hard to overcome those things and get moving in the direction God wants us to be going. Esther could have sat in the harem and let things fall as they would. She was in a hard spot, yet she didn't let it get her down. She didn't sit around comparing and thinking she couldn't do it. She showed a can-do attitude. She made the best of a bad situation.

It takes courage to have a good attitude.

Esther was no "Pollyanna." She did have to deal with the king's memories of Vashti. The beauty contest was held so he would forget about his former wife. Esther had one night to erase a whole marriage, or at least make him want to forget. That's a lot of pressure. She didn't give in to it.

As a senior pastor's wife, I feel the pressure to perform. I know there are expectations. I know that I'm expected to join in and lead ministry at some point. On the surface I'm okay with this, but my churning stomach and stiff neck tell me that deep down I'm feeling the pressure. Where's the pressure coming from? The truth? It's coming from my own expectations.

As they learned to write, my sons pressed hard on the page, so when they wanted to erase something it took several tries. Am I like my boys, going over and over a certain image, trying to make it disappear, only to have the paper left ripped and wrinkled and me frustrated and overwrought? I'm the one who's compared myself to what I think I am not. I've seen caring, compassionate women who in my mind would make a much better pastor's wife than introverted, sometimes cold fish me. I know I will fail to meet the people's expectations. It's only a matter of time. Can I accept the fact that I'm going to fail my own expectations because I've put them so high and based them on a mark I'm never ever going to meet? I should be more outgoing, I should be praying more, I should be taking a meal to that one, I should attend this—the mental list of shoulds is endless. I will never meet it. I'm not wired that way. Why do I think I should be?

I have a Vashti, and she's of my own creation. Yours may be the former pastor's wife, one of the stereotypes, a pastor's wife you watched growing up, your mother, or your mother-in-law. She may be a positive influence, or negative, or both. Who are the Vashtis in your life that you would like to forget but haunt you anyway?

That unrealistic expectation we're trying to erase is never going to be totally removed. It can't be. We need to accept that it's there but also acknowledge that we will never meet it. We are unique women. We need to embrace the differences and be who God created us to be. Who He wants us to be. That takes much courage.

BE A POSITIVE CHANGE

God created us as we are because He has a specific purpose in mind for each of us. Fulfilling that purpose will require courage, perseverance, and trust. It requires getting rid of all fear. It might be dangerous. Esther found this out after she became queen. Winning the beauty contest was not the end but rather the beginning. God wanted her in the palace as queen for a reason.

I followed my husband around the province of Ontario and then to a new province, New Brunswick. I didn't always like where we ended up. I would not have chosen some of those places. One time we moved to a big city so he could get his master of divinity degree. I hated that city. I confess, I never made the most of it. "Bloom where you are planted" is the old saying, but I didn't. I hated when people told me that. They weren't the ones planted in a detestable place! A place they didn't like! I didn't give it my all.

I find myself in a hard situation again. I'm trying to have a different attitude this time around, but it's hard. Some days I hate where we are living. My children are having a difficult time adjusting. I'm trying to teach them to "bloom where they are planted" too. I'm having a hard time because they're struggling. I'm trying to be more positive and show them that it will be okay. To be a positive change where we live.

"Be the change you want to see happen in the world." I want to see our neighbourhood change. So I'm trying. Being friendly is a good starting point. Some days that's all I can muster. I would rather hide than talk to the neighbours, so stopping and saying hi and getting to know them a little bit is a good place for me to start. I'm friendly with a little girl down the street who waits at the school bus stop. Her mom died a few months back. Saying "Have a good day" to her lets her know that I care and am thinking about her. It's the little things that can cause positive change. It starts with me and my attitude. I feel better about life and myself when I choose the better attitude.

Mordecai told Esther about Haman's plot against the Jews. At first she hesitated. If she went to the king as Mordecai proposed, it could mean her life. "All the king's officials and the people of the royal provinces know that for any man or woman who approaches the king in the inner court without being summoned the king has but one law: that they be put to death unless the king extends the gold scepter to them and spares their lives" (Esther 4:11).

Esther further explained that she hadn't been called by the king in a month. Maybe she lost his favour or he wasn't interested in seeing her right then. It was going to make it that much more awkward and dangerous to go to him. Mordecai fired back,

> *"Do not think that because you are in the king's house you alone of all the Jews will escape. For if you remain silent at this time, relief and deliverance for the Jews will arise from another place, but you and your father's family will perish. And who know but that you have come to your royal position for such a time as this?"* (Esther 4:13–14)

Who knows whether we have come to our places, our pastorates, our schools, and our neighbourhoods for such a time as this? Maybe we've been brought here to make a positive change in the lives of our congregations, our neighbours, and our kids. To start a revival in our homes and churches. To be overcomers. To show the world our courageous hearts even when our circumstances aren't so great.

Maybe our churches are in trouble, but we still need to be faithful to God. Maybe someone needs to see that example. Maybe it will just take one servant of God who's committed to obedience to turn that church around. I've seen it happen. I've heard stories of it happening.

Maybe my kids are struggling because they need to learn to handle difficult situations in a safe environment. So when hard times come later in life, they'll know who to turn to because they witnessed His faithfulness, His love, and His provision now. To risk for God means we get all the power and the fullness of Christ. We get the abundant life. I would much rather risk everything to make a difference and then experience hardship than to sit cowering in fear or, even worse, in smug indifference.

Esther risked it all to save her people. She approached the king after fasting and prayer. She didn't just dive in, but she went before the

Lord, fasting and praying for direction. She didn't just go on Mordecai's command. She went before God and asked. When the answer came, she took the leap.

When we get our answers, do we take the leap? Or do we sit back and doubt? A heart of courage takes the leap even though it may mean danger or a move from our comfort zone or comfort attitude. A heart of courage makes the leap like Esther did because it may mean for someone, perhaps someone we don't even know, the difference between life and death.

Chapter Seven

Restored

"Restoration matters to God.
The healing of the heart involves the healing of the past."
—Max Lucado

I make mistakes. According to my son, sometimes many. I mix up information. I choose the wrong size or style of clothing for my kids. I forget too much. Simple everyday mistakes. I also make bigger, more serious blunders. I open the door to temptation. I choose to lash out at my family and loved ones instead of calming down. I think unkind thoughts and judge rather than love. I am proud.

Unlike me, God doesn't make mistakes. When life is squeezing in on all sides, I find myself doubting this. Occasionally I've thought that He made a mistake in making me a mom. I haven't always had a stellar record in that area of life. *Wouldn't the boys have done better with someone else?* It's a lie that is whispered in my ear on days when I can barely keep my head up.

Other days I've thought that He made a mistake in picking me to be Mark's wife. I think I've come up short, so many times, in both being a wife and being a pastor's wife. Love doesn't always seem to win out. Anger and impatience do. Irritation because he doesn't do it my way, the *right way*.

Most Sundays, I'd rather stay at home than go to church. I feel like a fraud a lot. I'm a recovering people-hater. I don't usually know what to say in most situations. I'm useless at a funeral or in a crisis. I'm not touchy-feely. I like to be alone. These things are not qualities a person is looking for in a good pastor's wife!

Does God see it that way? Some Scripture leaves me scratching my head, wondering what God was thinking. Obviously He doesn't think like I do!

If you've looked at Jesus' genealogy, it may have been one of those times you thought God made a mistake. As in Rahab. A prostitute. Yet she was the great-grandmother of David, the greatest king the Jewish people ever knew. That's gotta be a huge mistake!

It's not. Does it make sense? No, it doesn't. It is more than my little brain can grasp, and it waters a small seed of hope. Maybe that's why I really like these stories of women who appear to be mistakes but are instead vital parts of the story.

Deep down I want to be like these women who are used by God despite their messes, mistakes, and warts. I don't want to be defined by my past. God used these women and their imperfections for His glory, and that gives me hope. We can all use encouragement on the days when our messes threaten to overwhelm us. Don't you agree?

Rahab was a prostitute, and it was precisely in that role—yeah, *that* one—that she was used to encounter the spies, to save them, and then to save herself and her family.

Commentaries agree that if you were new in town, you usually made your way to a public house. A prostitute's home. She knew people who knew information and the local gossip. If you wanted to find out anything about anyone, this is where you went. It wasn't just about sex. So Joshua's spies went to Rahab's home because they needed information, and it was the one place where they could stay undetected for a time.[41] Safe for the moment. But time was short. As soon as the king of Jericho found out that spies had entered his city he sent a message to Rahab to give them up (Joshua 2:3). Even the king knew where to look for "visitors."

Do I really believe that God made a mistake by using a prostitute to save the spies and help in the destruction of Israel's enemies? No, deep down I know there was no mistake. What really intrigues me is why. Why would God bother with a harlot like Rahab? How she made a living was sinful. Why didn't He just leave her be in her filth? The rest of civilized society didn't care about her. She wasn't worth the effort. Even in the king of Jericho's eyes, if she didn't do what he asked, he could easily get rid of her. She was expendable, not worth much. But in the eyes of the King of kings, she was a priceless gem.

What does that mean for me? For you? Perhaps in all our mistakes and messes and sin, maybe, just maybe, we are valuable too?

I heard author and teacher Beth Moore tell a story about how much God cares about those whom we consider trash. She was blown away. She asked God something like this: "Who are You? Who are You that You would do something like that?"

That question pierced my heart because in story after story in the Bible, Jesus took the time to care for the harlots, the down-and-outs, the adulterers, and the other undesirables of society. The sinful woman. The Samaritan woman at the well. The woman who was two seconds away from being stoned because the man she was with wasn't her husband. And Rahab. It makes me breathless! Hope extends its fingers to my soul.

In the Bible study *Eve & Rahab: Learning to Make Better Choices,* the author, Alice Mathews, makes this comment: "Again and again, we see the compassion of Jesus reaching out to women who had broken the rules and had lived lives that 'respectable' people looked down on."[42] It's not just a theme in the Bible; it's very much who Jesus is and how He still works today. It makes me want to weep. "Who are You, God, that You would care so much about those who will never measure up?" They will never be enough. People who are so far away from the perfection mark that it would take a lifetime to get even close. Their scarlet letters blind others to the person beneath them.

Truth be told, *I am one of them.* I have tried in vain to stop sinning, only to find myself right back in the same rut. I get angry. I yell. I get jealous. I get frustrated. And I get cynical. *Really? It's never going to change. You'll always be like this. You'll never change, so why try?* The lies go on and on. I despair. I start to agree with the lies. I live them out in a sick self-fulfilling prophecy.

Those women who caught God's attention stop me short. Rahab makes me wonder and think. She wasn't so far gone that she was past help. Things did change. She changed. God changed her. And she ran with it.

I can't change myself, but God can change me. The Creator can fix and restore because He made us in the first place. He can put us back together. He sees what we cannot: what He intended when He first made us in our mothers' wombs. "Rahab stands as a tribute to the possibilities within every one of us. God saw in her the possibility of an active and invigorating faith. Never mind what she was. *He looked at what she could become.*"[43]

REDEMPTION

That is the crux. God looks past the mistakes, the mess, and sees what we can be. What He *created* us to be and who He *wants* us to be. God saw who Rahab could be. Maybe Rahab, instead of looking at her circumstances, looked to what she could be with God's help. She believed in the foreign God, not only as *the* God but as the one who could help her.

Do I believe that God can help me? Do you? That He can restore us today?

Rahab had that kind of faith. She believed so deeply that she turned away from her sin and turned to God instead. He has great compassion. "As surely as I live, declares the Sovereign LORD, I take no pleasure in the death of the wicked, but rather that they turn from their ways and live. Turn! Turn from your evil ways! Why will you die, people of Israel?" (Ezekiel 33:11). Contrary to the popular world—and sometimes Christian—belief, God doesn't want anyone to perish. What He's looking for are people who will turn to Him and forsake all else, letting go of their pet sins, their excuses, and their fear.

God is compassionate, and He loves us. And we see this lived out in flesh and blood in Jesus and His encounters with humanity.

God is compassionate, and He loves us. And we see this lived out in flesh and blood in Jesus and His encounters with humanity. Because we are all Rahabs. We are all sinners. He has given us His power to change and to live victorious lives. The Holy Spirit living within us gives us this power. He is our guide and can help us change into the person God envisions us to be. He put Rahab in His Son's genealogical line. Hope takes its place beside Rahab in that genealogy in the opening chapter of Matthew's Gospel.

Grace was offered, and Rahab responded by turning to God and accepting that grace. She said to the spies, "When we heard of it, our hearts melted in fear and everyone's courage failed because of you, for the LORD your God is God in heaven above and on the earth below" (Joshua 2:11). This is a statement of faith. *The Expositor's Bible Commentary* says that verse 11 "is remarkable for a pagan and is evidence of her conversion to faith in Israel's God."[44] Rahab had heard the stories of God's deliverance of the Israelites from the Egyptians and the Amorites and *believed* them. She had faith that their God was capable of destroying the Canaanites because the Israelites were *His people*. She believed that He was God Almighty and no one was greater than Him.

Rahab was a Canaanite, an enemy of Israel. She was a harlot, which made her a bottom feeder in the chain of hierarchy. She had every reason not to trust in her enemy's God. Yet she did believe. Hers is a story of hope. Even more, a story of restoration. God took her heart and restored it to His. God is looking to do this exact thing for us, to bring our wounded, lost hearts back to His.

I find this story thrilling for exactly that reason. Hearts broken—abused, hurt, wounded, lost—made whole. It doesn't matter what's behind us, the messes, the mistakes! He takes it all and restores us to wholeness. He's just waiting for us to turn to Him. When our wounds leave gouges in us, we can do one of two things. We can try to bandage them, or we can take those deep wounds to Him to heal and redeem.

Many of us have had experiences where we have believed lies about ourselves. We are mistakes. We are bad. We have no worth. We will always screw up. For whatever reason, these messages have continued to play out in our lives. They have shaped us and defined us until we believe that's who we are. We filter our lives through these lies. These falsehoods steal our lives from us. As we turn away from these tapes and lies that whisper to us, we gain the upper hand. We see ourselves through Jesus' eyes.

I found that when I was able to get past the lies of my life, I was much more able to accept His love for me, which I hadn't been able to do before. When people or Jesus tried to love me, I could envision their love hitting me and bouncing off, away from me, like I didn't deserve it. I wasn't good enough to receive it, to keep it. Finally forcing that lie out into the light, I saw it for what it is: garbage.

I'm at the point now where I need to take this to Jesus' feet and leave it with Him to heal the wounds of my past completely. I'm on my way. Truths now have room to take root and bloom, truths about love, goodness, and mercy. They were all drowned out before by the lies. God is good, and He is shining through those gouges in me. I hope His light shines so brightly that people are drawn to Him. To His redeeming, restorative power. As Rahab was to this foreign God she had heard about.

God, in redeeming our pasts, uses every single thing for His glory. He doesn't waste anything; in fact, He turns it to abundance. Rahab heard the stories and believed. Her faith led her to save the spies from the king. She hid them on the roof and then redirected the king's messengers. She endangered herself and her family by doing this traitorous act. If the king had found out she had helped the spies, he would have had her killed.

FAITH AND OBEDIENCE

Putting faith into action usually means being uncomfortable. Not always, but many times it does. Being obedient doesn't come naturally to us. Oftentimes what God wants us to do doesn't come naturally to us either. Sometimes we want to be obedient, but the pain still has to be overcome.

I remember getting ready to move. The thought of telling the boys we were moving was painful. I wanted to run away from it. I didn't want to tell them. But it had to be done. Once the decision was made, we couldn't hide it or put it off. I literally felt a pain when I thought of it and their perceived reactions. And I wasn't far off. They didn't want to move. They reacted exactly as I had imagined. We believed that God was calling us to a new place—not just me and my husband but the boys too. It was part of His plan for all four of us. We had faith, and we acted on it.

Sometimes, as pastors' wives and ministry leaders, our faith requires more blind leaps of us than for others. We often are required to move our families to different locations. Locations that we may not want to go to. I've said *never* to a place, and—you got it—we ended up living there. It was where we were supposed to be, I believe, but that didn't make it any easier. Life is not a fairy tale, as society would have us believe. It's quite the contrary at times.

Oftentimes we are put in positions as pastors' wives that require a lot of faith, like Rahab was. Finances, time, and love all become for me like the oil in the jug of the widow from Zarephath in 1 Kings 17—commodities that are in very short supply but because of the miracles of God don't go dry! I don't always have the money, the time, or the love to do what I'm being asked to do, but I trust the one who does have all of those in abundance. There is always more than enough with God.

Taking the risk to be obedient is not a waste of our time or efforts. We may be planting the seed, or we may be blessed to see it harvested, but it's never in vain. We can still tell our messages of hope to others. We may never see the outcome—and that's okay. God is the restorer of hearts, not us. We only need to be about the business of living out His message of hope, restoration, and redemption.

It gives a new perspective to our lives and the roles we've been given. The Bible studies, the Sunday school lessons, the coffees and teas shared with other women are not wastes of our time. It's planting time.

Obedience means we don't give in to rebellion, jealousy, or fear, all of which can stop us in our tracks when we're following Jesus. Letting our spouses go out and follow their calls is a great sacrifice for each of us. God knew we could do it, which is why He called us to be the wives of our husbands.

It's super hard. I've found that if I let rebellion enter into my heart, obedience is much more difficult. Rebellion closes my heart up tight. I'm not willing to take risks for God or listen to His voice. We have the free will to choose to follow God's commands, but if rebellion is lurking, it usually hijacks our will and takes it captive so we make really bad choices. Rebellion moves us away from God, His love and His care. It's us who have moved away, not Him. It's hard to have a long-distance relationship with God. It doesn't really work.

Jealousy can be as destructive as rebellion. Remember King Saul and David? Jealousy made Saul a murder-breathing maniac. It can make me crazy too. All the comparing to other women and church leaders. Dissecting conversations and intentions. *What was she implying? What didn't she choose me?* The conversation in our heads can drive us crazy! It can also cause us to drop out of activities and ministries just because certain people are in them. We become uncooperative and unloving. It can make us egomaniacs too. There's no place for jealousy in the path of Jesus. I'm still learning this lesson. How about you?

Fear is the ultimate obedience killer. It's where rebellion, jealousy, anger, and all the other crappy things come from. Fear can paralyze you so you can't act. Fear can make you hide. Or it can make you angry, and you just come out swinging. For so long, that's been my go-to behaviour! The fear of not being enough, a mistake, is crippling.

Or maybe it's *inadequate*. I hate that word. It screams at me. I already know that I'm inadequate! I know that as a mom and wife. I chose those paths. Did we choose the path of a pastor's wife? Some of us did and some of us didn't. It's a little vague in my mind. If I wanted to marry the man I loved, then that path was chosen for me.

It's harder to accept my inadequacies. Why choose me when I'm bound to fail? There are so many other women better suited, I think to myself, who are more compassionate and kind-hearted. Who aren't so painfully awkward! Fear of not being enough lays me out. I will never be enough.

Maybe that's the point. Without God, I'm bound to fail. I am not enough. But we serve a God who is King of enough. Maybe it's not about doing a job but rather about drawing closer to the one who is able to help us—and will. But He wants us to come to Him in all our inadequacies. He already knows what they are. He wants a relationship with us. Do we want one with Him, or do we just want to do our job?

What stands out in my mind about all those women in the Bible who were second-class citizens, including Rahab, is that they wanted a relationship with God too. Yes, some were skeptical or suspicious at first, but they knew the real deal when they saw it. They grabbed hold of it as soon as they recognized it, unlike most of the first-class citizens, who were too busy doing their jobs or believed they didn't need any help. Rahab and the others were open to Him. Because of that openness and faith, Rahab had a relationship with the one true God.

She chose to make Him her God. Even though she didn't fit the prototype of a heroine of God's people, she had the faith of one. Isn't that what counts in the end? Even though I may feel like a mistake in this role, and in some of the other roles I fill, isn't it about my faith? Choosing to trust and have faith in someone bigger than myself? Choosing to follow down the hard paths even when I don't want to?

Rahab chose to hide the spies. She didn't have to. She could have opted for the easy way out. I don't believe for a single second that it was easy for her in any way. I want to live these stories myself, not just hear about them second-hand! To jump right in when God is telling me "Yes!" rather than cower in fear.

Fear never leads to obedience unless it's a reverent fear of God, a respect so that you trust Him even though you are afraid. The reverent awe of God trumps fear. I want to follow God more than I want to be safe. I'm willing to look down that particular gun barrel and stand my ground. I think Rahab lived that way, don't you? She faced the danger threatening her life and looked at God rather than the "what if" of being found a traitor to her king and people. In hiding the spies Rahab "sided with Israel against her own people. It was an act of treason!"[45]

Then she lowered that scarlet cord and saved herself and her family. It meant starting anew with new people. That's scary, isn't it? Starting out fresh with a whole new tribe! Maybe, like Rahab, we don't move physically, but the surroundings look a whole lot different. Even though she was in the same land, the Israelites were foreigners with foreign customs. Don't you think she felt like she had entered a whole new world? But God blessed her for her obedience and faith.

Obviously at some point Rahab must have married and had a least one child, as she's in the lineage of King David and, farther on, Jesus. God didn't just bless her; she was honoured. She's mentioned for her faith in the Hebrews' Hall of Faith (Hebrews 11:31) and again in the book of James (James 2:25). Rahab didn't just accept the invitation from God to change her life; she *embraced* it! She didn't let fear rule the day. She didn't let her past control her future. She believed, she acted, and she accepted all the grace that God gave her in abundance. She was restored.

Let's do a little heart check. How are we doing? Are we embracing the opportunities that God brings along or are we cowering in fear and mistrust and disbelief?

Do we get bogged down with all that's wrong in church? When things go awry, it can knock us out. A lot of people out in the world are questioning the relevancy of church. People aren't crowding into church; they seem to be running from it. It seems like a mistake too. Are we wasting our lives on something that isn't even relevant and is more a source of grief and pain than anything else at times? Really, what was God thinking?

I have to believe that church is not a waste of our lives. God did not make a mistake in building His church. Sometimes it seems like it might be. Sometimes I've wondered, why bother? It's never going to change. People are messy, dirty, and unlovely a lot of the time. They fight and don't get along. They take ownership of something that was never theirs to have, to control. It's God's church, not people's.

But God knows this, and still He sees His pure bride, not the tangled broken pieces of a steeple and all the messed-up people beneath it. A colleague and friend told us that God chose the local church as His main means of fellowship between believers. He's right.

So as a pastor's wife who truly believes in her husband's calling as well as her own, I choose to have hope that God will restore the church to her full glory. I choose obedience to a call that has caused at times great grief and at other times joyous victory. I choose to remain faithful to Him who is enough. I choose to work alongside Him so I can catch glimpses of His glory in His church.

You know those times. When we see Christ walk among us. When the elderly gentleman still takes care of his forgetful or sick wife. How he holds her hand as they walk into the foyer. The mom who comforts her child who fell off the curb rather than scolding or yelling at him, even though she told him three times to not walk on it. The child who lets another go first for his favourite game. These are sacred moments. It's these everyday moments that make it worth it. And then, of course, there are the extraordinary moments as well. And even those moments that are meant for evil, God turns around. He restores them. As Joseph told his brothers, "You meant evil against me, but God meant it for good" (Genesis 50:20 NASB).

No, the church is not a mistake. I am not a mistake, and neither are you. God, in His infinite wisdom and grace, knew exactly the plan He had for Rahab and for you and for me. And for His bride. It might not follow conventional paths. In fact, I'm sure it won't. Because for God it's not about perfection. He's already perfect. What He's interested in is our relationship with Him. In restoring our hearts to Him so we can have that relationship. And in that restored heart comes faith and obedience and a life lived out in abundance because He is enough.

Chapter Eight

Known

I went to a pastors' wives' conference, not knowing what to expect. I was thinking about the information I could get out of it, take home, and apply. A "to-do" list that would make me a better pastor's wife.

I was open to hearing God speak, but I was doubtful deep down that He would. I'd already taken up His time at another conference. He wasn't going to show up again. I'd get my to-do list and enjoy seeing Beth Moore in person. It was all I could expect, I thought. That, and the holiday away from the cares of being a wife and mom. I kept telling myself it was enough.

My friend and I spent the next two days in workshops on the ins and outs of being a spouse to a pastor. It was fascinating to see the differences in all our churches. There was a lot of take-away information but nothing really new. I was right. God wasn't really going to show up.

Beth Moore was to speak on Friday night and Saturday. I sat beside my friend and fellow pastor's wife as we waited for Beth to come out. We worshipped in freedom and safety. It was liberating to know that no one was watching and I could praise God how I wanted. We were challenged that weekend to "let our true hearts be seen; be willing to feel." That's what I wrote down in my notebook. I let myself be open to the idea of being willing to feel. It was a scary thought, but deep down, I wanted desperately to hear from God.

That night, Beth asked us to describe our lives in six words. It was our homework. I remember sitting in my hotel room, trying to figure out how to describe my life in six words. This is what I came up with: "Invisible and unloved, gripped by fear."

I'm not sure that at the time I understood where it all came from. I got the *fear* part, but *unloved* and *invisible?* What was that about? Now, seven years later, I know where those words came from. The Holy Spirit gave them to me because He knew, in God's timing, that those two wounds would have to be healed. Healing began that weekend, but it was going to be a long journey.

WHAT'S IN A NAME?

I had an issue with names. My name, to be precise. Very deep inside my soul, I felt nameless. Bible verses about Jesus knowing our names and the number of hairs on our heads would leave me in tears. I didn't understand why this was such a big deal.

I come from a large family. No one ever got my name right on the first try. Or second. It happens. Most parents do it. I only have two children, and I can still call them by the wrong name. Or my husband's name!

I'm a twin. Being one of two can be an identity crisis waiting to happen, even with a fraternal twin like me. My parents raised my twin sister and me as individuals. We don't look alike. She had blue eyes, and mine are hazel. We have totally different interests and talents and opposite personalities. I love my twin sister like no one else, and I love being a twin. The downside is that people often lump you together instead of looking at you as two separate and unique individuals. It can cause identity issues for some of us.

I was "one of the twins" or "one of the Arnott girls." I was never just me. I was always part of a group. It wasn't done to harm me. It wasn't even done in unkindness. It was just the way it was. What was wrong with me that I had a problem with it?

Since that conference, I've learned that there is something important about being called by your name. It gives ownership. It makes whatever is being said to you ten times more personal. You've got my attention when you call me by my name.

There's a particular encounter in the Bible that always gets my attention. Jesus had been crucified, and His body was gone from the tomb. Mary Magdalene was standing outside the tomb, crying (John 20:11).

If you didn't know the story well, you'd wonder which Mary the author was writing about. I remember that as a young girl I couldn't keep all the Marys straight; they would blend together. Why were all these important women in Jesus' life named Mary? His mother, Martha's sister, and Mary Magdalene. There were others. These are the ones mentioned the most. Talk about an identity crisis!

It makes this encounter with Jesus even more compelling. Her name is Mary. Like being a Jane Doe today. Common. Almost nameless. They added "Magdalene" on the end to distinguish her from the other Marys. She was from Magdala, a tiny fishing village near Capernaum.[46] *Mary Magdalene* is her moniker.

Mary doesn't leave the garden with the others. She turns and sees a man, who she thinks is the gardener. She asks him where they have taken Jesus' body. At this point Jesus calls her by her name, "Mary!" and then she instantly recognizes Him.[47]

The moment is thrilling. It touches me deeply. Jesus is so beautiful at this moment. By beautiful, I mean in His kindness to Mary. In His love for her, His compassion toward her. He calls her by her name when she is feeling lost, alone, and afraid.

How do you think He said it? Was it soft and soothing? Did it have an urgency to the tone? It was filled with love, I have no doubt. Instantly she recognized Him.

He called her by her name. I don't think he tacked "Magdalene" on at the end, either. She was Mary, and He knew exactly who she was, inside and out. He didn't need "Magdalene" to identify her to Him. She wasn't "Mary the insane one" or "the possessed one" to Him. She was Mary. Daughter of the King. Beloved. He knew all of her, including her past, present, and future. He understood her grief at that moment. Who is this Jesus? I want to know *Him*. I want to have that kind of relationship. Deep, personal.

Mary had a past. Still Jesus loved and accepted her, despite it. Many think she was a prostitute. There's no evidence to suggest that she was an immoral woman. What Scripture tells us is that she was possessed by seven demons (Luke 8:2). Jesus cast out those demons and healed her. That was her past—demon possession.

What is demon possession? We read about it in the Scriptures, but I'm not sure I ever really understood it totally. John MacArthur does a wonderful job describing what it is and what is it is not in his book *12 Extraordinary Women*. He writes, "Demon possession involves bondage to an evil spirit…that indwells the afflicted individual."[48] He writes that in every case in the Scriptures it is shown as an affliction, not a sin. It suggests a great deal of suffering.

Mary knew the meaning of suffering. The demons took their victims and ruined their lives. They were cast out of society. They were left alone to fend for themselves. It only took one demon to devastate a person. She had seven.

Can you imagine the kind of life Mary had? If you could call it a life. Interestingly, those demons never willingly entered or let their victims enter Jesus' presence.[49] So it can be assumed that Mary didn't go to Jesus for help. We aren't told how she came to be in His presence, but she did, and He released her from her captivity. It was no accident that she ended up in the same place as Jesus at the same time!

He knew all there was to know about Mary. It's not just about names. It's what those names represent. Mary was Magdalene, who had seven demons cast from her. That was part of her name. But it wasn't the end. There was Mary the beautiful. Jesus saw all of her, just like He knew all of her name. He saw her beautiful heart filled with love and devotion for Him and for His people. He knew her as Mary the servant. She served Jesus and His disciples while they ministered. She gave her own resources to further the kingdom of God. Jesus knew her as Mary, beloved. She was a daughter of the King of the universe, not for what she did but because she chose to accept that inheritance.

Jesus knows us like that. Every single thing. Scary, isn't it? And *still* He loves and accepts us. He knows the ins and outs of our lives, minds, and hearts. I'm not just Jennifer from Canada who's been a mess her entire life. My name means much more than that. I'm Jennifer of the Kingdom of Heaven, daughter of the King. Beloved. Lovely to behold.

Who has made plenty of messes but none that can't be redeemed by her Father. She's scandalously forgiven. She has graciously been given a seat at the family table. She is able and encouraged to approach her Father, the King, at any time. He's never too busy to listen. She's never invisible to Him. This is, in part, who I am to Jesus. Do I see myself the same way?

Because this is truth. Some of the other stuff is lies. Learning to tell the difference can transform our lives. Sometimes it's hard for us to believe the truth about our true identities because the lies have been told to us since we were small. You're not important. You're invisible. You're not worth it. You're a mess. You're bad. You're never going to amount to anything. Most of us know our identity lie, that one thing that continuously whispers in our ear. It's a destroyer.

Jesus wants us to know the truth, who we really are in relation to Him and how He sees us. I believe we have to really understand and believe that we are loved by the King before we go out and serve Him. Because in the end, we serve what or who we love, don't we?

Mary's freedom from the evil spirits was complete. "Her life was not merely reformed; it was utterly transformed."[50] Can you imagine how this turn of events changed her life? She was free to go back and have a life. Be part of a family again. Go to market. Enjoy life. But I think the transformation wasn't just about the demons. It changed her heart. She gave up her life to follow the one who gave it back to her. She became a disciple.

I used to think that she just cooked for the group. She helped meet their physical needs and with their costs of living and so on. Now I'm not so sure. I'm more inclined to think she was involved with the day-to-day ministry as well. She was a disciple of Jesus. He was her teacher. When she recognized Him in the garden she called him *Rabboni*, or *teacher* (John 20:16). You wouldn't call someone that if He wasn't that to you. Although the women probably did do the cooking and caring for Jesus and His band of twelve, as well as the others, I think they were also disciples, involved in ministry.

Living on the road with Jesus, witnessing His care and compassion, listening to Him teach, and then watching Him live it out would be a great way to get to know Him. Mary knew Jesus. He was her master as well as her teacher. Her Saviour.

He called her by her name, and immediately she recognized Him. If she didn't have any kind of relationship with Him, she would not have known His voice. But she did. Mary's friendship with Jesus was intimate. It went beyond Him healing her from the demons. That was the starting point, but Mary didn't just leave it at that. She joined His group and followed Him, both physically and spiritually. They were good friends. I want that kind of friendship with Jesus, the kind where I'll recognize His voice when He calls. When I am alone, afraid, and sad, His voice will penetrate through it all, and I will know Him.

When I am alone, afraid, and sad, His voice will penetrate through it all, and I will know Him.

Jesus and Mary had a deep, intimate relationship, but there was no impropriety between them. Hollywood and imaginations have taken this friendship and made it into something it wasn't. There's no evidence to even hint at any kind of inappropriate relationship here. Alice Mathews in her book *A Woman God Can Lead* writes,

> What we do know is that while Jesus' enemies accused Him of Sabbath-breaking, of drinking too much wine, and of associating too closely with tax collectors and other disreputable types, at no time did they ever raise a question about sexual immorality.[51]

The religious leaders were on the lookout for any hint of scandal concerning Jesus. They would have been all over even the slightest hint of immoral behaviour. No, this relationship between Mary and Jesus was one of love. A deep, holy, and pure love. The kind God intended when He created humans for relationship with Him.

Wouldn't you give anything to be able to live a few years with Jesus right there in the flesh beside you? I think then we would really know Him. But would we? Did Judas? We can travel and live with someone and still not know him or her very well. We have to make the effort to sit at the feet of Jesus and listen to His teachings, like another Mary did. We have to engage in conversation with Him. Ask questions, observe. Get near Him instead of hiding out in the back with the gang. Too busy with the tasks we *absolutely have to* get done. Too busy with other friends. Too afraid to step up and make a change. To let ourselves be vulnerable and come out into the light. To make ourselves visible. Telling ourselves that we'll have time later, not realizing that we have to make the time. It won't just magically appear.

It's no different today. He's not here in physical form, but we still have to play our part in our relationship. To participate in getting to know Him. The desire and commitment have to be there. Mary had that. She was dedicated to *Him,* not to *ministry*.

She has an important lesson to teach us as pastors' wives. Are we dedicated to Jesus or to ministry? Many of us, as well as those we serve, answer that question all wrong. We're dedicated to ministry more than we are to Jesus. We're more dedicated to ministry than to getting to know Him intimately. We have it backwards. Our hearts and minds should be His first. It's only from that love, that relationship, that healthy ministry will flow. What I mean by healthy ministry is service because we want to, not because we have to. Service because we want to follow Jesus wherever He goes and be involved wherever He has called us. Because we love Him so much and we can't get enough of Him. I don't think I'd mind ministry if it was like that.

I think it was like that for Mary. MacArthur writes, "Mary owed everything to Christ. She knew it too. Her subsequent love for Him reflected the profound depth of her gratitude."[52] I have to ask myself, does my life reflect my profound gratitude? Does my love exemplify my gratefulness? I think it would if I really understood who Jesus is.

I don't think I really do. Maybe that's why this story is thrilling and incomprehensible all at once. Who is Jesus? Would the real Jesus please stand up, because I think I'm only starting to actually see Him. The other Jesus, the cruel taskmaster, the one I chase but can't quite catch— that isn't Him. I've been serving a false god for a very long time.

Mary knew the real Jesus. She knew His character, that He loved His Father and He was all about doing His Father's business. But she also knew that He loved a bunch of ragtag fishermen like His own family. That He didn't just speak about a radical love; He lived it. He confronted the religious elite about their hypocrisy. While everyone else feared them, He didn't. He was kind and gentle to the most despised in society. He touched lepers and made mud to heal a blind man's eyes. He had patience that wasn't earthly.

I think the thing that clinched the deal for Mary was Jesus' love. If He'd been mean and cruel, a driven master and teacher, I don't think she'd have stayed around. She'd already lived that out with the demons that had possessed her. I know I don't want to serve that kind of god. It's exhausting. It kills on so many levels. I'd be worn out, not just physically but spiritually and emotionally as well. That kind of god drives people away. Jesus drew people to Himself, and they stayed because they wanted to.

In His presence, our identities fall into place. Beloved. Daughter. Son. Of the King. Lavishly loved. Accepted no matter what. *No matter what.* We might have demons in our past. We might be a walking train wreck right now. We might have really messed up. It doesn't matter to Jesus. He loves us no matter what. We don't have to do anything to earn that. Nothing.

Grace. Love. They're there for the taking. The only thing we have to do is realize how much we need them. Accept them. Let go of our pride. Because the only thing that's really keeping us from this gift of grace and love is our pride. Our desire to control our own destinies. We think we can play at being God. But it doesn't work that way. We aren't God. If we can get our pride out of the way, then grace becomes necessary. When pride is sent packing, there's room for love, both to receive it and to give it back. Mary did this so well. She knew Jesus, and because of this, she knew who she was in Christ. His beloved. Out of His love for her, she could serve Him with all her heart.

I've been asked to fulfill a calling. Not forced or coerced but asked. Called. Does my life reflect how grateful I am that He loves me so much that He died for me? That He has healed me and redeemed me? This calling He's asked me to fulfill isn't a punishment. He's trusted me with a role He thinks I'm perfect for and can do well. It's a tool He can use to teach me and whittle away some dead wood. Do I believe it? I don't.

Instead, I constantly complain about life or the church or my husband's job. I begrudge Him that calling. I have always looked at ministry as misery, a kind of perverse punishment for being bad. My identity has been wrapped up in a role and lies that I have fallen for and let define me.

Maybe it's time to get back to basics and ask a few questions. What do I believe about Jesus? What kind of relationship do I have with Him? Once I get that figured out, then I might be in a position to follow Him with abandon, with my whole heart.

If we truly understand how scandalous God's love is for us and how deep it runs, how can we not return that love? Mary did. Mary knew she was beloved, and it rocked her world. It changed everything. She didn't need to be told to serve. She didn't need to be talked into going along with Jesus and His disciples. She was already convinced, and so out of that love, out of that understanding, she loved back. She made sacrifices. She served not because she had to but because she wanted to. She knew she was loved extravagantly by an over-the-top kind of God, and that was all the motivation she needed.

I think I will only begin to fulfill my calling in life when I understand the depth of God's love. The extravagant price of it and how scandalous it was. I cannot force myself to love. I can tolerate for a while. I can fake it occasionally. I can lie to myself and stuff down my feelings. All for what? In the end, I hurt myself and my loved ones.

Eventually we burn out. We were never meant to do it all ourselves. To manufacture feelings. To use every last ounce of energy and strength to do what we think we ought to do. Serving out of a sense of duty is no way to live our lives, and it's not what God intended. He didn't want our relationship to be based on what we owe Him. I don't want that kind of relationship either.

At the end of that weekend in Nashville, Beth Moore asked us to again describe our lives in six words. On Friday night I had written "Invisible and unloved, gripped by fear." That weekend God let me know that in all the hardships, He had never let me go. He knew me. He knew my name. I now wrote, "Never let me go. Name known."

I didn't realize at the time that it was just the beginning. He knew my name, and I thought that was enough. But since then, He has shown me over and over that it's not just my name He knows. It's all of me. Every single thought, desire, dream, heartache, worry, need. Every single cell, He knows intimately. Deeply. Lovingly. And He's calling me, by name, into a deeper, more intimate love than any I can experience with anyone else. Now, years later, my six words would be "Name known. Loved deeply. His daughter."

Endnotes

INTRODUCTION

1   Beth Moore, *James: Mercy Triumphs* (Nashville, TN: Lifeway Press, 2011), 204.

CHAPTER ONE

2   Ethel Herr, *Chosen Women of the Bible* (Chicago: Moody Bible Institute, 1976), 12.

3   Herr, *Chosen Women of the Bible*, 16.

4   John MacArthur, *12 Extraordinary Women* (Nashville: Thomas Nelson, 2005), 5.

5   *Collins English Dictionary*, s.v. "coequal."

6   Frank E. Gaebelein, ed., *The Expositor's Bible Commentary*, vol. 2 (Grand Rapids: Zondervan, 1992), 46.

7   Gaebelein, *The Expositor's Bible Commentary*, vol. 2, 48.

8   Gaebelein, *The Expositor's Bible Commentary*, vol. 2, 45.

CHAPTER TWO

9   Donna Paulson and Norma Shirck, *Christ's Encounters with Women* (Philadelphia: Lutheran Church Women, 1973), 51.

10 Matthew Henry, *Matthew Henry's Commentary in One Volume* (Grand Rapids: Zondervan, 1961), 1375.

11 Paulson and Shirck, *Christ's Encounters with Women,* 52.

12 Henry, *Matthew Henry's Commentary,* 1375.

CHAPTER THREE

13 Henry, *Matthew Henry's Commentary,* 246.

14 Gary Inrig, *Hearts of Iron, Feet of Clay* (Grand Rapids: Discovery House, 1979), 65.

CHAPTER FOUR

15 *Collins English Dictionary,* s.v. "petulant."

16 MacArthur, *12 Extraordinary Women,* 27.

17 MacArthur, *12 Extraordinary Women,* 28.

18 MacArthur, *12 Extraordinary Women,* 38.

19 Gaebelein, *The Expositor's Bible Commentary,* vol. 3, 147–8.

20 MacArthur, *12 Extraordinary Women,* 29.

21 MacArthur, *12 Extraordinary Women,* 36.

22 Susan Miller, *After the Boxes Are Unpacked* (Carol Stream, Illinois: Tyndale House, 2016), 59–60.

CHAPTER FIVE

23 NIV Study Bible notes.

24 Henry, *Matthew Henry's Commentary,* 1436.

25 Henry, *Matthew Henry's Commentary,* 1436.

26 Alice Mathews, *A Woman God Can Lead* (Grand Rapids: Discovery House Publishers, 1998), 300.

27 Henry, *Matthew Henry's Commentary,* 1436.

28 Henry, *Matthew Henry's Commentary,* 1436.

29 Stormie Omartian, *The Power of a Praying Parent* (Eugene, Oregon: Harvest House Publishers, 1995), 74.

30 Mathews, *A Woman God Can Lead,* 300.

31 Jay Pathak and Dave Runyon, *The Art of Neighboring* (n.p.: Baker Books, 2012), 15.

32 Pathak and Runyon, *The Art of Neighboring,* 25.

CHAPTER SIX

33 Ann Voskamp, *One Thousand Gifts: Study Guide Video* (Grand Rapids: Zondervan, 2012).

34 *Collin's English Dictionary*, s.v. "palimpsest."

35 Timothy K. Beal, *Book of Hiding: Gender, Ethnicity, Annihilation and Esther* (London & New York: Routledge, 1997), 30.

36 Beal, *Book of Hiding*, 30.

37 Beal, *Book of Hiding,* 29.

38 Beth Moore, *Esther: It's Tough Being a Woman Bible Study* (Nashville: Lifeway Press, 2008), 41.

39 Moore, *Esther,* 41–42.

40 Charles Swindoll, *Esther: A Woman of Strength and Dignity* (n.p.: Thomas Nelson, 2008), 48–49.

CHAPTER SEVEN

41 Gaebelein, *The Expositor's Bible Commentary,* vol. 3, 259.

42 Alice Mathews, *Eve & Rahab: Learning to Make Better Choices,* Discovery Series (Grand Rapids: RBC Ministries, 2003), 33.

43 Mathews, *Eve & Rahab,* 34, emphasis added.

44 Gaebelein, *The Expositor's Bible Commentary,* vol. 3, 262.

45 Gaebelein, *The Expositor's Bible Commentary,* vol. 3, 260.

CHAPTER EIGHT

46 MacArthur, *12 Extraordinary Women*, 173.

47 MacArthur, *12 Extraordinary Women*, 173.

48 MacArthur, *12 Extraordinary Women*, 174.

49 MacArthur, *12 Extraordinary Women*, 176.

50 MacArthur, *12 Extraordinary Women*, 176.

51 Mathews, *A Woman God Can Lead*, 331.

52 MacArthur, *12 Extraordinary Women*, 177.